Meet the 7 Retirement Villains:

1. **LADY LONGEVITY:** Of course we all want to live a long, healthy life; but Lady Longevity puts an evil spin on our wish. Her goal is to try to make you ignore the possibility of a long life in your retirement plan, thereby leaving you penniless and without choices if you outlive your money! Truly evil!

2. **THE INVISIBLE ENEMY:** This photo is of one of the rare occasions he allowed us to see him – because normally he remains completely hidden. He is inflation, and his goal is to make things FAR more expensive the longer you live – ruining your retirement lifestyle!

3. **EVIL UNCLE SAM:** We all know that we need to pay taxes to the IRS, but Evil Uncle Sam goes a step further. He looks for all the different ways he can squeeze more and more money out of retirees. These taxes often don't affect the rich OR the poor. Instead, he goes after the people who work their whole lives to try to save for a comfortable retirement. You and me!

SAVE YOUR RETIREMENT!

4. SARAH SELF-PAY: Sure, our government provides retirees with Medicare; but what about all the types of illnesses Medicare *doesn't* cover? Nursing care can cost up to $7,000 a month or even more! Sarah Self-Pay's goal is to force you to pay ALL of that out of your savings…until there's nothing left!

5. ICEBERG IVAN: Ivan pulls the fees out of your savings and investments. Like the "tip of the iceberg," he tries to make sure you can't see them. His goal is to cost you hundreds of thousands of dollars during your retirement, all the while keeping those fees hidden under the surface and out of sight!

6. SYSTEMATIC SAMMY: Sammy poses as a financial planner and gives you what sounds like a logical plan for you to take income systematically from your nest egg during your retirement. Little do you suspect that his "plan" could destroy your nest egg faster than you can say "a wolf in sheep's clothing!"

7. ANTIQUATED ANDY: At first glance, Andy may seem harmless; but he represents outdated investment strategies that many Wall Street firms refuse to update. These strategies could expose your nest egg to many unnecessary risks. A true hazard to your *wealth!*

PAT STRUBBE

Save Your Retirement!

PAT STRUBBE

Out to Save Your Retirement From Mass Destruction By The 7 Retirement Villains!

4th Edition

The contents of this book are provided for informational purposes only and should not be construed as financial or legal advice. Before embarking on any financial or legal planning, be sure to consult with an experienced elder law attorney and financial advisor.

Securities offered through Arkadios Capital, Member FINRA/SIPC. Advisory services offered through Arkadios Wealth. Preservation Specialists and Arkadios are not affiliated through any ownership.

The opinions stated within are as of the date of publication and are subject to change. Information has been obtained from a third party sources we consider reliable, but we do not guarantee the facts cited are accurate or complete. This material is not intended to be relied upon as a forecast or investment advice regarding a particular investment or the markets in general, nor is it intended to predict or depict performance of any investment. Past performance is no guarantee of future results.

Copyright © 2024 Patrick A. Strubbe

All rights reserved. No part of this book may be used or reproduced in any manner whatsoever without prior written consent of the author, except as provided by the United States of America Copyright law.

ISBN: 9798874194772

DEDICATION

To my wife and children:

Janelle: Your unfailing love and commitment are my rock. Your support means the world to me.

Carter, Ava, Gabby, and Isla: You are the light of my life, and I grow more proud of you every day.

Contents

Foreword by Dawndy Mercer Plank	1
Introduction	3
Chapter 1: The REAL Reason Your Retirement Needs to be Saved!	7
Chapter 2: The Aging of America	17
Chapter 3: The Invisible Enemy	25
Chapter 4: Taxes: The Good, the Bad, and the Ugly!	39
Chapter 5: The Skyrocketing Cost of Healthcare	59
Chapter 6: Wall Street Greed	79
Chapter 7: Is *This* the Biggest Lie of the Brokerage Industry?	93
Chapter 8: Is There a Better Way to Invest?	109
Chapter 9: YOUR Retirement Income Plan	125
Chapter 10: Save YOUR Retirement!	139

PAT STRUBBE

x

ABOUT THE AUTHOR

For over 27 years, Pat's mission has been to help people retire with peace of mind. What started one-on-one with his clients now spreads to many through his books, television, radio, and podcasts.

In 2012, the first edition of this book became a best-seller on Amazon.com. It was named one of the '5 Personal Finance Books to Read in 2022' by Forbes.com and one of the 15 best personal finance books that will help you make smarter decisions with your money in 2023 by CNN.com. In March of 2021, he reached best-seller status again with his most recent book, "The Retirement Secret."

Pat is a recurring guest on the WIS-TV (NBC) news with anchor Dawndy Mercer Plank and is also the retirement expert on the weekly segment the "Midlands Retirement Report" on WIS-TV (NBC) as well as WLTX (CBS). He has been featured in USA Today, Investor's Business Daily, Entrepreneur.com, Columbia Business Monthly, and the Lexington Chronicle.

You can listen to Pat share retirement tips on his radio show "Save Your Retirement®" on WVOC-AM 560. You can also listen to past episodes wherever you listen to podcasts by searching for Save Your Retirement.

After growing up in Indiana, Pat graduated with honors from Purdue University and lives in Columbia, South Carolina, with his beautiful wife, Janelle. He is the proud father of four children: Carter, Ava, Gabriella, and Isla. Pat enjoys time with family and friends, including watching his lifelong favorite team, the Los Angeles Lakers. An active member of Hope Lutheran Church in Irmo, Pat has served as an elder of finances since 2003.

Foreword

By WIS NBC-TV Anchor Dawndy Mercer-Plank

My eyes usually glaze over when reading books about investing or protecting my money. I very much want to make the wisest financial choices, but let's face it – not all our brains are programmed to get excited about debt-to-equity ratios. That's why I'm glad Pat Strubbe has published his fourth edition of "Save Your Retirement!"

Pat's humorous examples and ideas take what could be perplexing points and puts them into practical, entertaining explanations. As an evening news anchor for an NBC affiliate in South Carolina, it's important to me that the expert guests I choose to put on my shows offer reliable advice in a variety of areas that help my viewers live better lives. One of those key areas of need deals with finances. After receiving a copy of Pat's book, I immediately wanted to schedule him as a regular guest on WIS TV News at 4pm as I saw he'd be able to offer helpful financial advice my viewers can understand. Pat covers the As to Zs of money for my viewers – from annuities to yields (is there a "z" financial word?). And in his newest edition, Pat educates and explains in such a way we can see dollar signs clearly through what otherwise could be cloudy financial concepts.

Dawndy Mercer Plank
Anchor
WIS NEWS TEN

dawndy@wistv.com // 803-758-1269
Ephesians 4:29

Dawndy Mercer Plank

Dawndy anchored WIS NBC News 10 at 4:00, 5:00 and 5:30 for 27 years. Her awards include Best TV Personality for 2023, 2017, 2015, 2014, 2013, 2012, 2011, 2010, 2009, 2008 and 2003 by Columbia Metropolitan Magazine. The Free Times Newspaper awarded her Best Anchor Personality for 2010, 2009, 2008, 2005, 2004, 1995 and 1994.She was a 2011 Palmetto Center for Women TWIN Nominee, an honor presented to women whose outstanding achievements mark them as leaders.

Dawndy's extensive coverage of a young boy's life changing because of a cochlear implant landed her a second place award by the Associated Press in the Medical/Health category in 2009. In 2002, the South Carolina Governor's Council on Physical Fitness awarded her its Media Fitness Award. Dawndy ran as a torchbearer for the 2002 Winter Olympic Games.In 1994, she received the South Carolina Broadcaster's Association Personality of the Year Award, as well as the National Journalism Award for Best Television Coverage of Leukemia.

Dawndy is a frequent speaker at churches throughout the state and is an active member at Shandon Baptist Church and is on the Oliver Gospel Mission's Vision Action Team. Dawndy is a board member of the Palmetto Center for Women and is actively involved in Trinity Focus, a monthly Christian outreach to businesspeople.

Dawndy Mercer Plank graduated with a BS in Telecommunications in 1989 from Ball State University in Muncie, Indiana, after an internship in Washington, D.C.

Dawndy is married to Craig Plank and has three stepchildren.

Introduction

I'll never forget the first time I saw the difficulties of handling your finances in retirement. I was 16. As you might imagine, retirement financial planning wasn't typically on my mind!

This story is about my friendship with my grandpa. He was my mom's dad, and since my grandmother had died when I was a baby, he had been a widower for many years by the time I was a teenager.

My grandpa was a farmer. While he'd served his country in the military for many years, including duty in World War II and Korea, I always knew him as a farmer. I was raised in northern Indiana, and grandpa lived in the southeast part of the state - a whole 'nother world to me!

My parents, sister, and I traveled down to southeast Indiana a couple of times a year to visit Grandpa and other relatives. I vividly remember that *every* time we saw my grandpa, we would take a walk on his farmland. He loved to do that. So we did – every time.

There's one specific moment I remember from when I was about four. A particular area of his land was completely fenced in, and we pulled up in our car to his gate. He couldn't open the gate that day, so everyone was climbing over it. It was about 5 feet high, but as soon as I saw my older sister climb that fence by herself, gosh darn it, I was determined to climb it too! When Grandpa tried to help me, I was adamant: "No, Grandpa, I can do it myself!"

Okay, I have to admit something here: I can remember that moment so clearly because my grandpa thought it was hilarious, and he loved to tell that story! Every time he did, we had a good laugh over it. Even now, it always brings a smile to my face.

By the time I was a teenager, my grandpa's health had declined considerably. After a series of mini-strokes, he couldn't live by himself anymore. There was no way he would ever consider moving away from his hometown, so moving in with us wasn't an option. That meant a nursing care facility.

As a teenager I was completely oblivious to anything related to the nursing care bills. All I knew was that instead of heading to Grandpa's house to visit him, we would go to his nursing care facility.

My Sixteenth Birthday

As he did on all my other birthdays, my grandpa called me on my 16th. We had a nice talk, and then he dropped his big surprise on me: he wanted to buy me a new car for my sixteenth birthday! Wow! I couldn't have been more excited! As much as I had appreciated all the previous years of birthday cards with a few dollars in them, you can imagine how much more excited I was about this!

After Grandpa and I were done talking, he spoke with my mom. She was a CPA and a very wise financial person, and she was handling all my grandpa's bills.

After she finished the phone call, Mom sat me down, looked me square in the eye, and told me that Grandpa couldn't buy me a car. I was in disbelief! How could I go from no expectation of a car to a promise of a brand new car, back to no car in less than an hour?!

I couldn't understand why there was a problem. As far as I knew, my grandpa had never had any financial issues. If he says he will buy me a car, why wouldn't he be able to?

This is when I got my first lesson in working with finances in retirement. My mom explained that my grandpa had never had money problems before his health declined. He lived comfortably in "retirement" for many years, with income coming in from Social Security, his military pension, and income from his farm.

But when Grandpa had his medical problems, his financial situation changed overnight. His monthly expenses skyrocketed. And while he had plenty of assets (his farmland), he didn't have an endless supply of cash in the bank. Not only are nursing care facilities costly, but it's also often difficult to predict future costs that might arise. Plus, his house was on his farmland, so there were still monthly expenses for its upkeep.

It was hard for the family to deal with my grandpa's health problems. But that's when I realized just how hard it was to deal with the financial difficulties, too. On top of figuring out everything concerning healthcare for my grandpa (from a long distance, no less), my mom had to deal with the stress of managing his finances and assets to pay for his nursing care and other monthly bills.

My grandpa passed away when I was in college. I started school as an accounting major because I knew I liked math, and I liked money. ☺ But his situation always stayed in my mind. I was fortunate to graduate from Purdue University during a strong economy, and I had five job offers to pick from.

I chose to help people with their finances, and after two years of devouring all the basics, I found a mentor to teach me all about the details of helping people as they plan their retirement and throughout their retirement. Since then, I've focused on being the best planner focusing on the retirement years I can be.

In my twenties, I thought I was lucky to have found my career so quickly. Now I realize there was no luck involved. God blessed me by showing me my calling and my passion, and that passion is why I wrote this book.

You see, there's nothing I get more satisfaction out of than when I make a difference in a client's life. But I believe that as challenging as retirement planning is today, it will only get more and more difficult. Over the coming pages, we'll talk about why in more detail. In his influential book *But What If I Live?*, author Gregory Salsbury, Ph.D. sums this up very well:

> *"Every successive generation of Americans over the last century has been more prosperous and has enjoyed a better quality of life and a better retirement. Every generation has seen an improvement – until now. But at the same time, retirement didn't used to be a problem – until now. To paraphrase a line from Oldsmobile, 'This is not your parents' retirement.'" The trouble is many boomers don't seem to know that retirement, if we have one, may be inferior to their parents', yet no one seems worried. And no one is taking action."*

Mr. Salsbury is right. Now more than ever, Americans need straight talk on where they stand financially, and they need help getting where they want to go. That's why I love what I do, and that's why I wrote this book. I hope that it helps you Save *YOUR* Retirement!

Chapter 1

The REAL Reason Your Retirement Needs to Be Saved!

Ohnosis: Realizing that you really should have started planning for retirement years ago.

Retirementology, by Gregory Salsbury, Ph.D.

In 1974, the Employee Retirement Income Security Act (ERISA) was passed.[1] This law birthed the IRA (Individual Retirement Account) and set the groundwork for all of the various accounts we now know as "retirement accounts."

The intent of ERISA was to encourage us to save for our retirement. You could say that a simple summary of ERISA's goal for us was for each person to have three areas to lean on in retirement:

1. Social Security
2. A Company Pension Plan
3. A Worker's Savings

These three are often referred to as the "3 legged stool of retirement planning." In September of 2020, researchers Dan Doonan and Tyler Bond published their paper titled "The Growing Burden of Retirement" which made some important observations about this subject:

> *Under the traditional retirement model of the "three-legged stool," guaranteed monthly income from Social Security is one leg of the stool; guaranteed monthly income from a defined benefit pension is another; and saving forms the third. This is the ideal scenario that was more commonly available to previous generations. While retirement planning would certainly be easier with two guaranteed income stream from Social Security and defined benefit pensions, the three-legged stool now is elusive for most American. NIRS research found that only 6.8 percent of current retirees received retirement income from all three of these sources.*[2]

Let's back up and take a good look at this. So before ERISA, a successful retirement depended on Social Security payments and your company pension plan. It sounds pretty straightforward. It also sounds pretty secure. In fact, you could say that an employee could retire and confidently expect their check to be in the mail. But with the introduction of the retirement plans that ERISA paved the way for, now *we* are responsible for a portion of that security.

The author makes an interesting observation: companies realized that these very retirement plans provided the opportunity to reduce or even eliminate the expensive pension plans they had been providing. And who can blame them? Dropping pension plans saves companies billions of dollars every year. When ERISA was passed, we were told it was to benefit employees. However, employ*ers* have benefited in a lot of ways. In many cases, the expense of retirement has been transferred from the employ*er* to the employ*ee.*

The Incredible Disappearing Pension!

Maybe you're thinking, "Oh, I'm sure it's not that bad - maybe just a couple of big companies that have done away with their plans." That is, sadly, far from true. Take a look at the number of active pension plans. In 1985, 114,396 defined benefit plans were active. [3] In 2022, that number had dropped to approximately 5,000.[4] That's a remarkable drop of 95%!

Why are these companies doing this? Because they need to, and because they can!

Because they need to: Many corporate pension plans are underfunded. So how does the company fix that problem? They can pour piles of money into their pension plan, or they can weasel their way out of making the payments. Which of these options do you think they'll choose?

Because they can: Numerous companies have already succeeded at reducing or completely eliminating their pension commitments. So, a company with a problem today can learn from those who have had that problem (and used this solution!) in the past.

The most widely known option is declaring bankruptcy. It's happened time and time again over the past two decades. A large corporation declares bankruptcy. Part of this process is pleading with a bankruptcy judge to allow the company to void its union contracts. One primary reason for this? To reduce or eliminate the existing pension commitments!

But wait, you say, doesn't the government have a program to protect us from these evil companies trying to weasel their way out of their pension promises? You're right. The Pension Benefit Guaranty Corporation (PBGC) insures most defined benefit pension plans.

However, I'm sure you know this program has its limits like anything else.

The 2022 PBGC Annual Report states that for the year, they paid out over $7 billion in benefits to more than 960,000 retirees.[5] As more pensions fail or are shut down, more and more pressure will be placed squarely on the PBGC.

The bottom line is that there is no reason for us to believe that the PBGC will be able to cover all the reduced and eliminated pension benefits. They actually can't typically pay the full benefit anyway. In some cases, *benefits have been cut by 60 to 70%!* So much for being insured!

What About Public Pensions?

Sadly, corporate pensions aren't the only ones with huge problems. At the end of 2022, the Center for Retirement Research at Boston College reported that the average public pension plan holds assets that are less than 74% of the current value of future liabilities.[6] That means there's, on average, a 26% difference between what they **should** have to cover those pensions and what they **actually** have.

The Council of State Governments confirmed that this shortfall at the end of 2022 was $1.3 trillion. They also report that several states are hovering at only having about half of their needed funding. These states include Illinois, Kentucky, New Jersey, and Connecticut.[7]

Sadly, states aren't the only ones with problems. Many municipalities have the exact same issues. In the April 4th, 2011 issue of Bloomberg *BusinessWeek*, Roger Lowenstein reviews various public pensions in his article: "The Great American Ponzi Scheme." (Yes, the title of the article is referring to public pensions!). Lowenstein reports that

Prichard, Alabama, was forced to stop sending retirees their checks in 2010.

But we were supposed to have a three-legged stool, right? Once they take away the pension leg, we're down to two legs. Oh, and that's assuming we trust Social Security. Yikes! We went from an idea of 3 legs to 2, one of which is wobbling badly.

Social Insecurity

I'm sure you've heard repeatedly about the problems with Social Security, but this is a *real* problem and warrants attention. Let me quickly make a few points.

First, the government is brilliant at making it sound like we've been "saving" all the excess taxes to fund Social Security over the years. They make it sound like our Social Security taxes go into a Social Security Trust Fund, but this couldn't be further from the truth.

Instead, part of the taxes received are used to pay current Social Security benefits. The remaining tax revenue is put into the general revenue fund for use as the government sees fit. There are NO assets in a trust fund – therefore, there is NO interest on the trust fund. This tax revenue is accounted for by the Secretary of the Treasury issuing an IOU for the amount used in the general fund. By the end of 2022, the U.S. government owed the trust fund approximately $2.8 *Trillion*. That's not a made-up number from someone making projections. That comes straight from the 2023 Social Security Trustees Report![8]

Ready for more bad news? Original projections had us believe that Social Security revenue would be greater than expenses until around 2016. It turns out we hit the mark a little sooner than expected…in

2010! The title of analyst Michael Barone's article in the *Washington Examiner* says it all:

"Social Security Cash Flow Suddenly Negative"

Social Security tax receipts for the first half of 2010: $346.9 billion; Social Security benefits payments for the same period: $347.3 billion. Before this year, projections have always been that Social Security wouldn't cross that line into negative cash flow for five years or so. Now it's a reality. Congress has been spending Social Security's positive cash flow for years. Now there's no positive cash flow to spend.[9]

So, what is the only leg left? Our savings. And do you know what is one of the craziest parts of the whole situation? What ERISA ultimately did was force millions of employees to become professional investors and financial planners – requiring us to build our savings on our own...without providing us with the financial education needed to plan successfully! Instead of finding a way to educate investors, the politicians have left the job of financial education up to the people of Wall Street.

Does that sound like a good idea? I think best-selling author Robert T. Kiyosaki of *Rich Dad, Poor Dad* fame said it best in his book *Rich Dad's Prophecy*:

"Asking Wall Street to provide financial education is the same as asking a fox to raise your chickens."

But that's what we're forced to do. After all, when you were in school, you were taught all kinds of things, right? Maybe you were taught Latin, for example, or trigonometry, or studied Shakespeare.

But when and where did anyone teach us how to plan for our financial future? Who taught us how to deal with the actual financial issues we face today?

It doesn't matter if you're a blue-collar worker, a business owner, a top corporate executive, or anything in between; most of us are not taught how to take care of ourselves financially. Nor are we taught how to plan for taxes and inflation, how to figure out what we need to do to meet our goals, or how to deal with the reality of paying mortgages, bills, tax problems, wildly fluctuating stock and bond markets, cash flows, budgeting, insurance, long-term care, health care costs, and on and on and on.

Our school systems don't deal with these issues. So, let's go back to Robert Kiyosaki's comment:

"Asking Wall Street to provide financial education is the same as asking a fox to raise your chickens."

Who is the fox Mr. Kiyosaki is referring to? That would be many of the financial salespeople you run into. Amazingly, stockbrokers from some of the biggest brokerage firms in the United States have even said they are not financial advisors or planners but merely commission-compensated salespeople whose primary job is to sell financial products! Where did they say this? *In sworn testimony!* (The brokers sued their employers under the Fair Labor Standards Act. Under Fact Sheet 17M, stockbrokers are entitled to overtime pay if their primary duty is selling financial products.)[10]

Interestingly, at the same time these stockbrokers are saying they're just salespeople, the brokerage industry is spending billions of dollars every year on advertising; and what titles do they use for their representatives in those ads? Here's a sampling:

- Financial Advisor[11]
- Investment Advisor[12]

It sounds like the brokerage firms don't think it would come off very well if their advertisements said something like: "Come in and meet with us – we've got the best salespeople in the country!"

The U.S. Securities and Exchange Commission has taken a stand here as well. They require all brokerage statements to display this message:

Your account is a brokerage account and not an advisory account. Our interests may not always be the same as yours. Please ask questions to make sure you understand your rights and our obligations to you, including the extent of our obligations to disclose conflicts of interest and to act in your best interests. We are paid both by you and sometimes by people who compensate us based on what you buy from us. Therefore, our profits and our salespersons' compensations may vary by product and over time.[13]

We should all beware of the fox chasing after the chickens!

Mr. Kiyosaki has one other piece of advice I must pass on:

"The point I want to reinforce is the idea that you as an individual have 3 basic choices:

(1) Do nothing,

(2) Follow the same old financial planning advice of diversify, or

(3) Get financially educated.

The choice is yours. Obviously, I recommend long-term financial education."

I couldn't have said it better myself! I hope you now understand **why** your retirement needs to be saved. That's why I wrote this book. Over the last 25 years, I've met with thousands of people to discuss their retirement plans. It pains me to see so many who aren't prepared.

Instead of giving you a boring textbook on steps to protect your retirement, what follows is a story. It includes:

- A couple planning for retirement: Dick and Jane
- Their friends who have already successfully planned for their retirement: Tommy and Brenda
- Seven retirement villains who you will meet throughout the rest of this book, and, of course,
- Our superhero: SuperRetirementPlanner

What did you expect: Superman? ☺ I hope you enjoy it, and I hope you plan and retire with confidence!

END NOTES

1. www.DOL.gov/ebsa
2. www.nirsonline.org/wp-content/uploads/2020/09/The-Growing-Burden-of-Retirement.pdf
3. "The Really Troubled Program," *Time* magazine, January 4, 2005
4. Public Plans Data National Data Overview, publicplansdata.org/quick-facts/national/#
5. www.pbgc.gov/sites/default/files/documents/pbgc-annual-report-2022.pdf
6. Public Pensions Contend with Falling Markets and Rising Inflation, crr.bc.edu/wp-content/uploads/2022/08/IB_22-13-2.pdf
7. www.csg.org/2023/05/03/unfunded-pension-liabilities-the-growing-cost-of-retirement/
8. www.ssa.gov/OACT/TR/2023/
9. "Social Security Cash Flow Suddenly Negative," *Washington Examiner*, June 12, 2010
10. The Lies About Money, Ric Edelson, 2007
11. fa.smithbarney.com/
12. www.totalmerrill.com/TotalMerrill/pages/accolades.aspx?pageurl=THE_BUCK_GROUP
13. The Lies About Money, Ric Edelson, 2007

Chapter 2

The Aging of America

By 2030, the demographics of 32 states will resemble those of Florida today.

Gregory Salsbury, PhD, *But What If I Live? (2006)*

Our story begins on a beautiful sunny day in Metropolis. Meet residents of Metropolis, Dick and Jane. Dick is 60, and Jane is 58. Jane works part-time as a receptionist at a dental office. Dick is an engineer who enjoys his work, but he dreams of having the freedom to do what he wants when he wants. So, he is planning feverishly for retirement.

Dick has spent the last few years devouring *Money* magazine, CNBC, the money section of *USA Today*, and personal finance articles he has found on Google. He has studied his pension benefits from his employer, poured money into his 401k, and estimated his social security benefits. Overall, he's a do-it-yourselfer, and he's done a thorough job in many ways.

Dick has decided it's time to show his plan to Jane. They sat in their den where Dick had been working and re-working his numbers for years. "Honey," Dick started, "I've crunched all the numbers, and the great news is, between my pension, our Social Security benefits, and a 5% withdrawal per year out of my 401k, we will be able to retire in two years when I turn 62!"

Jane responded, "That sounds wonderful, but how can you be so sure? Do we know your 401k will last?"

Dick put his hand on Jane's. "Absolutely. The numbers show that even if my 401k doesn't earn anything, it wouldn't run out for 20 years!"

"Well, I guess that sounds pretty good," said Jane.

Just then, a large cloud of smoke appeared in their den! Dick and Jane heard the loud sound of an older woman laughing. It almost sounded like cackling! As the smoke faded away, they saw the woman and couldn't have been more shocked! She was definitely older than they were. Their eyes focused on the regal-looking long red robe and crown she was wearing; perhaps most alarmingly, she was holding a long wand with a nasty-looking snake wrapped around it. "Who in the world are you?" Dick demanded.

The woman replied, "I am Lady Longevity! My goal is to have as many retirees as possible underestimate how long they will live and ultimately run completely out of money! I am here because I heard about your retirement plans, and I have great news! Well, I have great news for **me**. You see, your plan has an excellent chance of failing!"

"Failing? What do you mean?" asked Dick in a panicked tone.

Lady Longevity smiled. "Oh dear. You have no idea, do you? Let me be blunt. Failure means broke. If you live too long, you run out of money. You don't have enough to pay your bills. Do you know how people joke about not wanting to eat cat food during their retirement? My goal is to make sure you *have to*!"

Dick and Jane looked at each other. They were dazed and confused. Jane finally broke the awkward silence. "We don't want to go broke. Is this really such a big risk?"

"Look, most people can picture themselves growing old, relatively healthy, enjoying time with loved ones. Outliving your money is absolutely a real problem. You see, people are retiring earlier and they're living longer. It doesn't take a math wiz to realize that means we need to cover more income in between!

We all know we're living longer on average these days, but the *amount* of the increase is startling: life expectancy in America in 2022 was 76.4 years, while it was only 47.3 years in 1900."[1]

"Wow!" Jane exclaimed, "That's a staggering difference!"

"Absolutely," Lady Longevity continued, "According to the Bureau of Labor Statistics, a healthy couple in their mid-60s have a 50% chance that one spouse will live beyond their 91st birthday.[2] That means this couple has a 50% chance of needing at least 26 years worth of income – and of course, it could be many more years than that!

For his book *The Retirement Myth*, author Craig S. Karpel interviewed Robert N. Butler, M.D., on longevity. Karpel wrote:

> *"Robert N. Butler, M.D. is one of the world's most distinguished authorities on human aging. His 1975 book Why Survive?, exposing what he called "the tragedy of old age in America," won the Pulitzer Prize. "The longevity revolution is one of civilization's most extraordinary achievements. People are generally underestimating the number of years they're going to live, and what those additional years are going to cost them financially. The result is that they're underfunding their old age.""*[3]

Dr. Butler points out that living longer creates two problems: not only do we have to generate income for a longer period than many expect, but those years could be some of the most expensive of our entire lives."

Dick sighed. "I guess I didn't plan for all that. It's kind of depressing."

"Alright!" Lady Longevity said proudly, "It's always my goal to make people depressed – you just made my day!"

Dick went from "kind of depressed" to angry. "The feeling is definitely NOT mutual!"

Dick's anger made Lady Longevity smile even more, so she asked, "May I continue?" Dick and Jane nodded.

"And of course, most wish to retire earlier and earlier," Lady Longevity continued, "As recently as World War II, the average retirement age was 70. Now it's 61.[3]

But the truth is that early retirement is not always by choice. Whether forced early retirement is due to health reasons or downsizing, the unexpected effect on a retirement plan can be devastating.

In fact, according to Dallas Salisbury of the Employee Benefit Research Institute, 45 percent of Americans retire sooner than they had planned – half of those because of illness or disability.

Gregory Salisbury, Ph.D., sums up this problem perfectly in his book *"But What If I Live?"*

> *"A large portion of these people will be making an erroneous, and perhaps dangerous, assumption. Americans are suffering a common misperception that they will select their own schedule for retirement. ... But the reality is that two out of every five Americans won't have a choice of when they retire, because of health issues or job changes."*

So not only are we living longer, but we often stop earning income early – whether it is planned or not!"

Lady Longevity paused here for effect. "Have you ever had a life insurance agent give you a sales pitch?"

Dick sarcastically replied, "Unfortunately."

Lady Longevity ignored his comment and continued with her final point, "At some point, he will most likely ask you a question such as, 'What if something happens to you?' Now that we are living so much longer, the smart question to ask is, 'What if something **doesn't** happen to you?'"

At that moment, Lady Longevity knew her work was done. She had sufficiently depressed both Dick and Jane. So, with a swift wave of her wand, a puff of smoke engulfed her, and she disappeared.

Dick and Jane stared at each other dumbfounded. All Jane could muster was, "What do we do now?"

Dick hemmed and hawed. "WELL?" Jane demanded.

"Weeellll…" Dick finally admitted, "Remember when Tommy from work retired a few years ago?" Jane nodded yes. "Well, he told me that he never would have tried retiring without the help of a superhero. He said there are **seven** different **retirement villains** that would try to ruin your retirement. He thought the only way to protect yourself from them was with a superhero."

"Why in the world did you never share this with me?" Jane demanded.

"Honey, when you hear the superhero's name, I know you will agree with me – it sounds ridiculous!" Dick said in a desperate attempt to defend himself.

"Dick, you listen, and you listen good," Jane was ready to get on a roll! "You and I know that Metropolis is filled with villains and superheroes. If seven different villains are going to try to sabotage our retirement, you've got to be out of your mind to ignore the help of a superhero, and I don't care HOW silly his name is! So what is it?"

"SuperRetirementPlanner," Dick finally said.

"SuperRetirementPlanner?" Jane asked. Dick nodded yes. "I admit this is a pretty lame name, but regardless, we obviously need his help! You know what that means."

Dick knew immediately: "We need to go talk to Tommy!"

END NOTES

1. Centers for Disease Control and Prevention, https://www.cdc.gov/nchs/fastats/life-expectancy.htm
2. www.NewYorkLife.com
3. "What Is the Average Retirement Age in the U.S.?", July 18, 2023, https://www.nerdwallet.com/article/investing/social-security/average-retirement-age-us#

Chapter 3
The Invisible Enemy

"IT'S CALLED INFLATION"

Dick's friend Tommy lived nearby. He was relaxing in a rocking chair on his front porch when Dick and Jane pulled into his driveway. They drove in so fast that the screech of their tires almost made Tommy drop the lemonade he had been savoring.

"Dick, is that you?" Tommy asked as his old friend jumped out of his car.

"Yes, it is! Please tell me you have time to talk to us right now!" Dick exclaimed as he and Jane hustled to the front stoop.

Tommy smiled. "Sure. Brenda went to visit her family, so I've got nothing but time. Y'all look like you've seen a ghost!"

Jane opened her mouth to answer, but Dick beat her to it, "I think we just did – a crazy old lady with a wand and smoke just gave us the strangest and scariest talk of our lives right in the middle of our kitchen – and then she disappeared!"

Tommy couldn't hide his smile. "Let's see…crazy old lady…holding a wand…disappeared in a cloud of smoke…that sure sounds like Lady Longevity."

Jane was faster than Dick this time, "Yes, that's right! How did you know?"

"Jane, I'm so happy you're here," Tommy started. "I know because I retired a few years ago. I've met Lady Longevity. I've also met *six* other retirement villains in short order. Scared the life out of me, I don't mind telling you!"

"But why didn't you tell us about all this back then?!" Jane demanded.

Tommy wasn't surprised at all to hear her say that. "Jane, I **did** tell Dick. He refused to believe me. He said he thought he could figure it all out on his own. But the fact that Lady Longevity visited you tells me your plan isn't complete yet – in fact – it means your plan has a good chance of failing."

Jane was getting increasingly upset the more she heard: "Failing is exactly what Lady Longevity said! Tommy, I don't want to be broke in retirement. Is your retirement going alright? How do we make sure ours is safe and secure? Please help us!"

Tommy wanted to calm Jane down, so he moved towards her. He could stay calm, as this wasn't the first time his friends had approached him after being introduced to one or more of the retirement villains. "Jane, please settle down. Let me answer those questions one at a time. My retirement is going wonderfully. Brenda and I couldn't be happier. It's funny. When we met the retirement villains, we were terrified. But now we're so confident we sleep like happy babies!"

Jane had to jump in, "THAT'S what we want! How do you do that?!"

"I'll tell you exactly what I was taught: before you can solve the problem, you have to identify it," Tommy explained. "So tell me, how many of the retirement villains have you met so far?"

Dick and Jane could quickly see where this was going. "Just Lady Longevity – just now," Dick said.

"The path to a retirement without worry begins with meeting the other six retirement villains. Unfortunately, you two already look like you've had more than you could handle today." Tommy knew they would want to learn more as soon as possible, but he wanted to hear them say it.

"No!" Dick and Jane exclaimed – and Dick continued, "We're ready for answers – no matter how painful they might be." Jane nodded her agreement.

"Great!" Tommy responded, "That's what I needed to hear. Did you bring your retirement plans and notes with you?" Dick nodded yes and handed Tommy a manila folder. "Perfect, then we can get you on your way. Let's sit down at the dining room table."

The three of them sat down at the table. Dick and Jane sat next to each other – they had to because Dick was holding Jane's hand tightly and wasn't going to let go. He could sense they were about to go on the ride of their lives.

Tommy opened their folder on the table and then looked up. "Okay, I've helped quite a few friends through this process, and I think I know the most logical order to follow. Is it alright if I lead the way?" Dick and Jane quickly agreed. "Good. Let's look at your notes. I see that your income plan gives you the same income every year in your retirement; is that right?"

Dick knew what Tommy was suggesting and immediately defended himself: "Yes, I did that intentionally. I know things could get more expensive during our retirement, but I figured as we get older, we won't be as active, so that we won't be spending as much money each year. So, yeah, the income plan is the same amount each year."

Just then, a cloud of smoke appeared near the table. Dick and Jane shouldn't have been surprised, but they were. They both jumped out of their seats a little. But then they settled in and remembered why they were there. Once the smoke cleared, they assumed they would see someone. Except this time, they didn't.

"I don't get it!" Dick bellowed, "I thought we'd see the next retirement villain."

Tommy smiled. "You're going to meet the next retirement villain, but you won't see him! You see, he is rarely seen, and I have no doubt he will keep you from seeing him today." Naturally, Dick and Jane couldn't have been more confused!

Just then, the empty chair at the end of the dining table moved slowly away from the table and then stopped. Tommy said, "Hello, Invisible Enemy, I was expecting you."

"I know some people weren't expecting me!" A voice came from the chair. Dick and Jane were frozen. At first, Tommy laughed. Then, he began to lose his patience with their new guest.

"Would you please introduce yourself? Do you really enjoy scaring people that much?" Tommy asked.

"One of my favorite things in the world!" The Invisible Enemy responded, "Hi, Dick and Jane, my name is the Invisible Enemy, and I'm here because your retirement plan could lead you to failure. Of course, that's exactly what I *want* to happen!"

Dick looked at Jane and said, "I can't believe I'm about to talk to an empty chair!" Then Dick turned to the chair. "Okay, Invisible Enemy, we're here because we trust our friend Tommy and are ready to hear the truth. Please explain our problem."

The retirement villain looked over at Tommy, who was nodding in agreement. "Very well," he said, "here's your problem. The Invisible Enemy is all around you. NO ONE escapes it. It doesn't just affect retirees, but **every** single American.

So, why am I so commonly ignored if I affect everyone and am all around you? Because I'm sneaky! Most people don't notice me until it's too late to plan!

So what is the Invisible Enemy? I'm inflation. Another way of saying it is that the things you buy increase in price over time.

Does anyone escape inflation? Absolutely not! I wipe out your purchasing power at any income level. I am definitely a non-discriminating villain!

And I am most certainly a terrifying villain when combined with longer lives! Back around the time when Social Security was established, it wouldn't have been unusual for someone to retire at 65 and pass away before they reached 70. Inflation in retirement wasn't a problem.

But how about someone who retires at 62 and passes away at 92? That's a **whole** different situation, isn't it? How about a quick example to show how this works:

Let's say a 62-year old needs $50,000 per year to live on today. And for the sake of this example, let's say inflation grows during their retirement at 4.8% per year each year.

By the time our retiree passes away at 92, to keep her spending the same would require her income to be *$200,000 a year!* That's a big deal!

And that's why you **can't** skip the topic of inflation. The Invisible Enemy must be identified and dealt with!

So you might think this would be a big concern to many people. That's definitely not the case! Many people SuperRetirementPlanner meets with have no plan for it and aren't worried about it. Most of their previous advisors never even addressed it.

I'm sure Lady Longevity quoted Dr. Gregory Salsbury, Ph.D.'s book, *But What If I Live?* Here's another great one:

"If you forget about inflation altogether, its effect on your retirement lifestyle can be catastrophic. And yet very few people ever stop to consider the severity of inflation's impact."

Can you guess why so many ignore inflation? Because inflation is The Invisible Enemy. I hope you're catching the theme here!" Dick and Jane nodded yes emphatically.

"So let's look at just how bad inflation typically is." The Invisible Enemy continued, "Since 1914, inflation, as measured by the CPI, averaged 3.38 percent per year.[1] But does CPI really tell us how much prices are increasing? Many experts don't think so.

The government developed the Consumer Price Index (CPI) in 1913 to tell the public how high prices have gone up on average over a month's period. It's then converted to an annual rate of inflation. For example, the government might say that this month, the CPI went up 0.4% (4/10 of 1%), translating to an annual inflation rate of 4.8%.

Now, what's the problem with the CPI? First, the government uses only a limited number of items to calculate the CPI. So, the result doesn't necessarily reflect the reality of what you're facing when you buy things day-to-day.

For example, our government report might report that there is NO inflation. Therefore, Social Security benefits won't be increased. Yet you can't help but notice that during the year, your groceries cost maybe 10% more than the previous year, and depending on the day you're paying 25% more at the gas pump! That's not what *'no inflation'* is supposed to feel like!

Another problem with the CPI is that because it is based on a formula developed years ago, it doesn't necessarily mean the formula is correct, nor does it take consider all the variables faced today.

Because so many things revolve around how the government reports inflation to you, this can cause serious problems.

Jeffrey A. Hirsch says it well in his book *Super Boom:*

> "The U.S. Department of Labor's Bureau of Labor Statistics (BLS) has tweaked and manipulated the Consumer Price Index (CPI) so many times over the past 30 years or so in an attempt to mask inflation that the indicator may very well not detect a true upsurge in inflation in the years ahead."

I referenced the long-term average of 3.38% per year just a minute ago. That's what Uncle Sam says. But is that how our spending power has been affected?

If you want to talk about a difference between what Uncle Sam says, and what reality says, let's see how nursing home costs have risen. In 1964, the monthly cost of a top-end, high-quality nursing home was about $250 a month. Yes, you heard me correctly!

$250 a month in 1964. Over $7,250 a month in 2021 in Metropolis. By the way, costs are about the same here as in the Columbia, South Carolina, area. In some urban areas, the prices are over $13,000 a month![2]

How about gasoline? Remember when gas was only 29 cents a gallon? Today (2023), it usually costs over $3 a gallon.

I could go on making examples all day, but you get the point: what the government tells you about inflation and what it really is are two different things.

They are so different that many feel that CPI is a meaningless piece of information. The numbers don't lie. Whatever they are, they are. If the government wants to attempt to soften up this problem, that's its choice. But you know that whatever it costs to buy things is what it costs."

The Invisible Enemy had one final point that he wanted to sink in. "The bottom line is that there is more inflation than you realize. If you don't plan for it, your retirement plan isn't going to work."

Dick had a worried look on his face and sighed, "I think I'm starting to see how I had this wrong."

An Invisible Enemy Example

Tommy then said, "Go ahead and give them an example."

"Very well," the Invisible Enemy replied. "When Grandma Margaret's husband passed away, he left her with a relatively modest pension from the railroad, a Social Security retirement benefit, and an almost-paid-for home.

In 1965, when she retired, she was receiving a little over $400 a month. She had about $15,000 in the bank and a mortgage payment of only $97 a month. Her other fixed expenses, such as food, utilities, insurance, health costs, etc., only ran about $175-200 a month.

At that time, Grandma Margaret had a small surplus cash flow each month (around an extra $50 a month), money in the bank, and a very secure and peaceful retirement in front of her. Or so she thought!

Over time, things really changed. Grandma Margaret was in excellent health, and ten years after her retirement, at age 75, she still had basically the same $400 a month coming in. But her expenses had increased to the point where she was spending more than her income each month.

But she was able to just barely make it. She moved into a retirement home. (She refused to sell her home as all the kids had grown up there, and she wanted it to stay in the family.) Her monthly expenses were up to around $700 per month. This negative $300 per month in cash flow didn't seem too bad since she had funds in her bank account to cover the shortfall.

Now we move ahead ten years to 1985. Grandma Margaret is 85, still in good health, and in financial trouble. Her bank accounts are at zero. She's living in the retirement home, still in decent health but failing, and having to depend on the grandkids to put in money each month to pay her bills and take care of her.

If she needed anything, the family had to buy it for her. The $400 a month she was getting at age 65, which seemed OK at the time, was nowhere near enough at age 85!!

Grandma Margaret committed the sin of enjoying good health and believing she would be okay in retirement, but in reality, The Invisible Enemy inflation had wiped her out."

Over the last few moments, Jane let out an audible gasp. Even though this retirement villain was invisible, she could see clearly for the first time and was scared. She could see herself in Grandma Margaret's shoes. The Invisible Enemy continued:

"See, Grandma Margaret didn't realize how bad things were because she was living her life day-by-day and didn't see the jumps in prices all at once. For example, currently, gas is $3.00 a gallon. In 1971, if you had told someone who wasn't very familiar with inflation that gas would run $3.00 a gallon, they would have thought it would be too expensive to drive a car.

If you had told that person in 1971 that their $20,000 house would be selling for over $180,000 today, they would have thought you were crazy! Heck, in some places, that $20,000 home now sells for more than $300,000!

That $3.00 gallon of gas we bought today, based on an inflation figure of 5% per year, will cost us $4.88 in ten years and $7.96 in twenty years. Imagine it costing $200 to fill up your car!

The car you bought for $30,000 with a monthly payment of $450 might cost $50,000 with a monthly payment of $750 ten years from now and more than double that in twenty years. Can you imagine paying $1,500 per month for a car payment to get an average, nothing-fancy type of car?

Well, it's no easier for you to accept paying that high monthly car payment than it was for Grandma Margaret to accept that her $97/month mortgage payment would turn into a $700/month fee at the retirement center for her to have a place to live. The prices we live with and accept as "normal" would have made Grandma Margaret think you were loony tunes if you told her what things would cost.

She wouldn't have understood how anyone could survive with prices like that, and as it happened, she didn't survive financially. She lived in her 1965 mentality You had better stop thinking those things aren't possible because they will become a reality. Slowly and surely, your budget will increase."

Dick had heard enough, "So, what do we do? How do we deal with inflation?" Dick asked.

Although no one in the room could actually see him, The Invisible Enemy had a huge smile. "As far as I'm concerned, DON'T!"

Tommy, however, knew that the Invisible Enemy had provided everything he needed for Dick and Jane's lesson. "Thank you, Invisible Enemy. Dick, Jane, and I will now make a plan to protect them from **you**!"

"I refuse to sit around and watch **that**!" A cloud of smoke appeared, and there was now quiet at his end of the table.

"I hate to assume," said Jane, "but it appears the Invisible Enemy has left."

Tommy laughed. "Yeah, I guess he could be tricking us, but I know he was telling the truth. He couldn't bear to watch us create a plan to protect you from him."

Dick was too worried to laugh. "So I know I've already asked, but how *do* we protect ourselves from him?"

"It's actually straightforward," Tommy responded. "SuperRetirementPlanner."

Dick looked dejected. Jane jumped in, "Oh, yeah, you mean the guy who can protect us from Lady Longevity too, right?"

"Yes!" Tommy exclaimed, "So Dick **did** tell you about him?!"

"Oh yeah, he told me about him, alright," an exasperated Jane said. "He told me about him right before I told him to get our butts over to **your** house!"

Tommy let out a big laugh. He had seen this before. One spouse didn't let the other in on the situation until they absolutely had to. "You came here and asked me how to protect your retirement from these retirement villains. Well, SuperRetirementPlanner is the way. You asked how Brenda and I are enjoying such a peaceful retirement. SuperRetirementPlanner is the reason why. A good retirement planner can be your superhero and help protect you from these villains. But I suppose you might like to know a little about how he will do that, wouldn't you?"

Dick and Jane nodded emphatically.

"Okay, here is a quick and simple summary of what he did for us and what he'll do for you. First, he ensures you realize that you **need** a plan for inflation."

Dick interrupted, "After some quality time with that invisible dude, that is NOT a problem!"

Tommy smiled. "I figured as much. The next thing he will do is have you figure out your monthly budget in today's dollars and come up with a realistic number of how much after-tax income you need to live on today, right now."

Dick jumped in – again! "Okay, I admit I messed up this retirement plan, but at least I have that part figured out!"

"Good!" Tommy said. He figured Dick had taken enough abuse for now and could use some encouragement. "Then he will help you estimate how much income you will need and want in retirement. Since you're not yet retired, this can be quite a challenge, but even if you're taking a guess, it's still a valuable process.

You have to pick one or more inflation rates and see how much this same monthly budget will cost in the future so you can have the same lifestyle throughout your retirement – and, most importantly, protect you from running out of money!

By this point, you can see an accurate estimate of what type of income you will need each year throughout your retirement. You can then compare these numbers with how much monthly income you expect from sources like Social Security and any pensions. There will likely be a difference, and that is what you'll have to generate with your nest egg.

Generating that income from your nest egg is **far** more complicated than most realize, and we'll get to that when we visit with another villain."

"There are still five more, right?" Jane asked.

Tommy was glad Dick and Jane were paying close attention: "That's right – and they're all important. So, I think we've covered The Invisible Enemy enough for now. We should move to the next villain when you two are ready. Just never forget that people live a lot longer now, which makes the effects of inflation even worse. The longer you live, the more time there is for inflation to eat into your savings!

The only true answer is to plan. Monitor your plan, update your plan, and make adjustments as necessary so you're always on target and you don't ever end up like Grandma Margaret."

Dick and Jane looked at each other. Then Dick said, "Don't worry, we definitely don't want that either. And I'm sure I speak for Jane when I say, we want to keep meeting these villains as soon as possible!" Jane nodded in agreement.

"Great," said Tommy, "Then let's keep rolling!"

END NOTES

1. www.tradingeconomics.com/united-states/inflation-cpi
2. https://www.genworth.com/aging-and-you/finances/cost-of-care.html

Chapter 4

Taxes: The Good, the Bad, and the Ugly!

"The hardest thing in the world to understand is the income tax."

Albert Einstein

"Okay, we've talked to Lady Longevity and the Invisible Enemy. Who's next?" Jane was now on a mission and wanted to discover what else she and Dick needed to know.

Tommy smiled, "Alrighty. Dick, I'm looking at your retirement plan and don't see anything about taxes. Did you give that much thought?"

"Not really," Dick replied, "I figured taxes are taxes, so they wouldn't be much different when we retire."

The moment he finished his sentence, a large cloud of smoke appeared. Dick and Jane were briefly startled, but as you might imagine, they were getting used to this type of thing. Once the dust settled, Dick and Jane saw an old, wrinkled man with white hair and a long beard standing across the room from them. He wore a blue and white striped blazer, bright red pants, and a large, red, white, and blue top hat, and he had a crazed look in his eyes.

"I WANT YOU!" He said as he lurched forward, pointing his boney finger at Dick and Jane. None of the previous villains had physically approached them, so they naturally jumped back.

"Want us to what?" Dick asked the man as clearly as he could muster.

Tommy knew he needed to introduce everyone. "Dick and Jane, I want you to meet the next retirement villain. Please say hello to Evil Uncle Sam."

Before Dick or Jane could say anything, Evil Uncle Sam said, "You know I hate it when you call me evil. Why can't you just call me Uncle Sam?"

Tommy wouldn't let him play the sympathy card: "Knock it off, Sam. You're as evil as they come! You don't want Dick and Jane. You just want their money – and lots of it!"

Tommy turned his attention to Dick and Jane. "Uncle Sam used to only stand for good. But Evil Uncle Sam represents everything wrong with our government and their spending. Since the politicians can't and won't control their spending, they have to tax us at every possible turn. That's what this man represents."

Evil Uncle Sam didn't say a word, so Dick spoke up: "Okay, so we have to pay income taxes during retirement. Is that all this is about?"

Tommy sadly shook his head. "Oh, if it were only that simple. Evil Uncle Sam, it's time for you to give them the truth. Tell Dick and Jane about taxes during retirement, and don't leave anything out. Tell them the good, the bad, **and** the ugly."

Evil Uncle Sam gulped. "Everything?" He asked hesitantly. Dick, Jane, and Tommy all nodded their heads yes. "Okay," Evil Uncle Sam started, "I hate to admit it, but taxes are an even bigger deal than most Americans realize. Did you know that taxes are the average American's largest expense? It's almost twice as much as the second-highest category, which is housing. In 2019, combined federal, state, and local taxes made up 29% of the average American's income."[1]

"That's ugly," Dick interjected.

"Well, I do have to tell the truth," Evil Uncle Sam replied. "And that's just the bad. Here's the ugly: It's quite possible that this is more important than at any other time in our country's history. Just ask anyone if they think future tax rates will be higher or lower. With our government racking up massive deficits year in and year out, most find it hard to imagine a way to avoid tax increases."

As he made this point, Evil Uncle Sam pulled out some slides from the inside breast pocket of his jacket.

Federal Debt Held by the Public, 1900 to 2053
Percentage of Gross Domestic Product

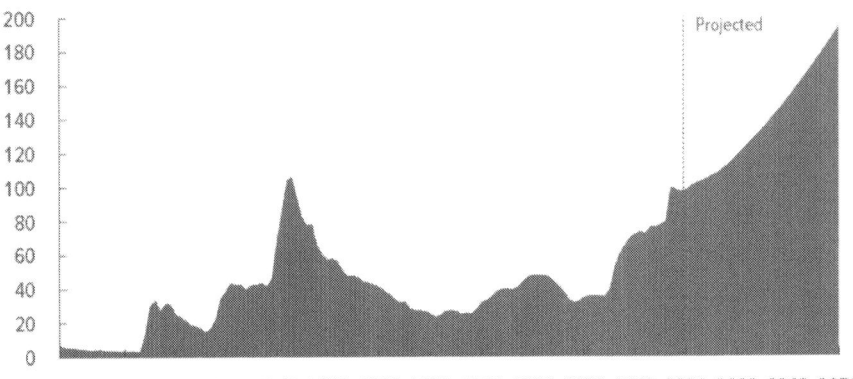

Figure 4.1[2]

"You brought visual aids?" Jane couldn't resist asking.

"I make him bring them because I think people learn much easier that way," Tommy said with a smile.

Evil Uncle Sam rolled his eyes: "Take a look at Figure 4.1. Do you want another reason to fear higher income taxes in the future? While we pay massive amounts of taxes in all areas of our lives, the income tax has been much worse at different times over the last one hundred years. Check out Figure 4.2.

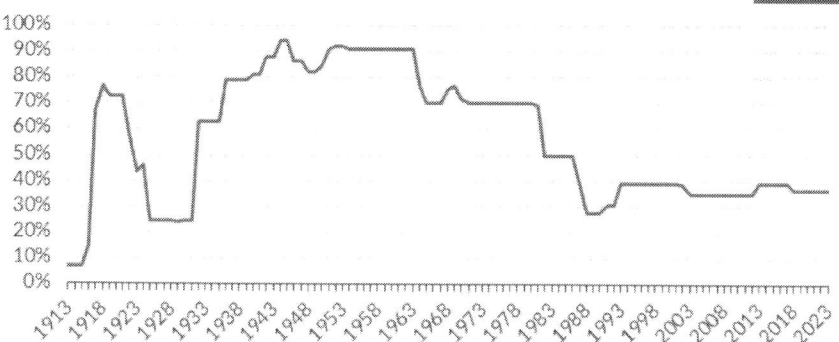

Top Federal Individual Income Tax Rate
1913-2023

Figure 4.2[3]

As you can see, the highest income tax rates have been MUCH higher than they are now. So, there is a historical precedent. The bottom line is that government is spending out of control, and it's hard to find any expert who doesn't think taxes are going up. So what does that mean for you? It means you need to plan to lower your taxes now AND attempt to lower them in the future!"

Lowering taxes was music to Dick's ears. "I promise you I am ALL for that!"

Evil Uncle Sam continued, "You should realize that what you do in one area of your financial life will affect all the others. Nowhere is this more true than with taxes. I can't think of a single thing you can do financially that does not affect your taxes.

If you keep your money in the bank, that affects your taxes.

If you take your money out of the bank and put it somewhere else, that affects your taxes.

If you sell stocks, that affects your taxes.

If you buy or sell a house, that affects your taxes.

If you set up certain trusts and wills for your estate, that affects your taxes.

If you make gifts, that affects your taxes.

If you have a part-time or full-time job, that affects your taxes.

If you own a business, that affects your taxes.

Every activity, financially speaking, will be reflected somewhere on those tax forms. Since tax planning and investment planning are so intertwined, they must be coordinated so every decision you make will be integrated with the other areas of your financial life.

Another issue has to do with tax law changes. They come at us fast and furious! This is yet another essential reason to have an advisor, as well as to ensure your advisor stays up on changes. Just because your planning today is legal and to your advantage, it won't necessarily be that way in the future. Therefore, you need to review your tax planning periodically to make any necessary adjustments."

Tommy sensed Evil Uncle Sam stopping. "If that all makes sense, I'm going to have Sam explain a couple of his nasty tax traps to you, and I'll teach you some of the basics of avoiding those traps that I've learned from SuperRetirementPlanner!"

Jane scribbled her pen on her notepad to ensure there was plenty of ink for notes. Dick, happy to let Jane do all the note-taking, leaned back with a huge smile. "Music to my ears!"

Part 1: Reduce or Avoid Taxes on Social Security Benefits

Evil Uncle Sam hated Tommy's attempts to help people. Still, he couldn't resist sharing the gory details of his tax traps, so he immediately started, "One of the biggest mistakes retirees make is overpaying income taxes, which includes the additional income taxes caused by Social Security income. It's like there are two different tax codes in America: There is one while you're working, and there is an entirely different one when you are retired. Taxation of Social Security benefits is definitely one of the driving reasons.

Let's start at the beginning. FDR established Social Security in 1934, and a promise was made that it would never be taxed. Sadly, politicians paid no attention to that promise…"

"BIG surprise!" Dick couldn't help interrupting.

Evil Uncle Sam rolled his eyes again. He hated that part of his talk because it always seemed like someone interrupted! He continued, "1984 is when Social Security benefits were first taxed. Then, the amount of your Social Security benefits that could be taxed was increased in 1993, and now up to 85% of your Social Security Benefits may be subject to tax.

Some have called the taxation of Social Security benefits a "tax on the wealthy." This is because when it was started, it is estimated that only 10% of recipients were affected. However, that has now increased to over half of recipients![4]

How is that possible? Well, the income limits put in place in 1984 have never changed. As people's incomes go up with inflation, more and more pay this tax every year. So, a tax initially intended to target only the wealthiest of retirees now affects the bulk of the middle class as well."

Dick was mad. "Tax on the wealthy, my…" he started, but Jane wouldn't let him finish. "Uh, honey, you're right. That's clearly not fair. Let's let him continue." Dick leaned back in his chair. He had a lot he wanted to say, but he bit his tongue.

"Thank you," Evil Uncle Sam said, "So taxation of Social Security benefits costs many retirees as it is and isn't going to get any better. Let's look at how it works and some ways to try and avoid it. Let's start with Don and Joan."

"I hope you like this example," Tommy interjected, "It was my idea. I like examples. Plus, the cool part is they are real people, and it shows their real situation. They live right here in Metropolis!"[5]

Example: Don & Joan

Social Security:	$66,000
Pension:	$31,200
Interest Income:	$36,000

Based on the 2023 Federal Tax Rate Tables, married filing jointly, two exemptions and standard deduction.

Figure 4.3

Evil Uncle Sam rolled his eyes yet again. "As you can see from Figure 4.3, Don and Joan are comfortably living off a pension, Social Security, and income from their nest egg. Please keep in mind everyone has a different income in retirement.

So, whether your income might be higher or lower than theirs, the process still applies.

Don and Joan are happy with their income, but they want to lower their taxes. Have you ever heard the idea that you won't pay much in taxes in retirement?"

Dick and Jane both nodded.

Evil Uncle Sam loved sharing this part: "Well, that's certainly not always the case. In federal income taxes alone, Don and Joan pay almost $10,000 annually, but that's not all. Some find the effect of taxation on their Social Security benefits to be downright shocking: every time they make an additional dollar, they now have to pay taxes twice. Many call this the retiree double tax.

Let me give you a simplified example. Let's say Don and Joan's bank raises their interest rate just a little bit, and they make one extra dollar in their savings account this year. Of course, when they make an extra dollar, they have to pay taxes on it. They are in the 22% tax bracket. Therefore, they owe $0.22 of income tax on the extra dollar. But their Social Security benefits trigger an additional tax. For Don and Joan, this is another $0.19 tax on the extra dollar.

So Don and Joan made an extra dollar, and they had to give back 41 cents in Federal taxes. At this time, the highest tax rate in America is 37%.[6] So even the wealthiest people in the country, like Bill Gates and Jeff Bezos, are paying no more than 37% on taxes. Yet here we have Don and Joan, middle-class retirees, paying 41 cents on that extra dollar."

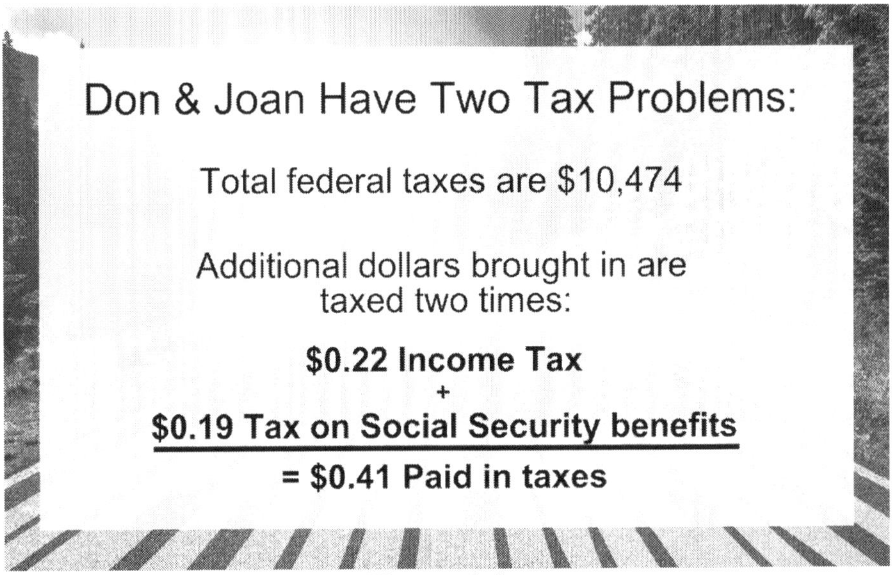

> **Don & Joan Have Two Tax Problems:**
>
> Total federal taxes are $10,474
>
> Additional dollars brought in are taxed two times:
>
> **$0.22 Income Tax**
> +
> **$0.19 Tax on Social Security benefits**
> = **$0.41 Paid in taxes**

Figure 4.4

Dick was downright angry. "Wait a second! All those rich CEOs with private jets and yachts and ten different houses all over the world are maxed out at 37% taxes, and regular retired folks like Don and Joan have to pay as much as 41% in taxes on some of their money?! That's not just unfair. That's criminal!"

Tommy nodded in agreement. "I couldn't agree more. I have no doubt you understand why this process is so important. We need to ensure your plan gives you every chance to avoid this stuff."

"It better!" Dick replied while leaning back and crossing his arms.

Evil Uncle Sam took that as his cue to continue. "It's clearly not fair, and with regard to Don and Joan's Social Security and pensions, there is no planning you can do to change how they affect their Social Security taxation. We can only work with their income from their nest egg.

Fortunately for me, almost all your savings and investments will help trigger this taxation. This includes any kind of bank or credit union accounts like CDs, savings accounts, and money markets. If you have a retirement account and are withdrawing money from it, it also contribute to the Social Security taxation.

The same is true of stock and mutual fund dividends and capital gains. Rental and bond income are included as well. Even tax-free bond interest is included!" As he said these things, Evil Uncle Sam had a smile on his face for the first time. In fact, it was a devilish grin.

Tommy had seen this look way too many times. "Hey! You're not here to brag about how you get money out of people – you're here to tell them how this works."

Evil Uncle Sam, you guessed it, rolled his eyes and then said, "Fine, then. If you don't like how I explain it, YOU do it!"

"I thought you'd never ask!" Tommy said in a huff, "So the only types of investments that can help you avoid this taxation are anything that has either some kind of tax deferral to it or creates tax-free income. Some examples would include:

- A retirement account you are not withdrawing from,
- Deferred Annuities,
- Some Income Annuities,
- Savings bonds,
- Some real estate investments, and
- Tax-free income from Roth IRAs and some life insurance."

Evil Uncle Sam was visibly irritated. He knew where this was going, and Tommy was happy to press forward, "Do y'all want to see how

SuperRetirementPlanner helps so many retirees reduce the taxation on Social Security benefits?"

Dick and Jane both leaned forward. Dick answered first (as usual): "Jane is ready to take notes!" Now, it was Jane's turn to roll her eyes.

Tommy was excited to continue. "He uses an idea called Tax-Advantaged Income. This type of planning looks very different for different people in different situations. You can set it up before you need the money and take it later, or you can set it up and start taking income immediately. So it depends on your personal situation.

Also, to really go into it, we would have to get into all kinds of IRS documents. Because of those reasons, I don't go into the nitty-gritty of how it works. I'll just show you what it does for you. The goal is to see if you can reduce or eliminate taxation of Social Security benefits."

Solution:
Tax Advantaged Income™

Federal taxes: $3,200/year

Additional dollars brought in are taxed two times:

$0.12 Income Tax
+
$0.10 Tax on Social Security Benefits
= $0.22 Paid in taxes

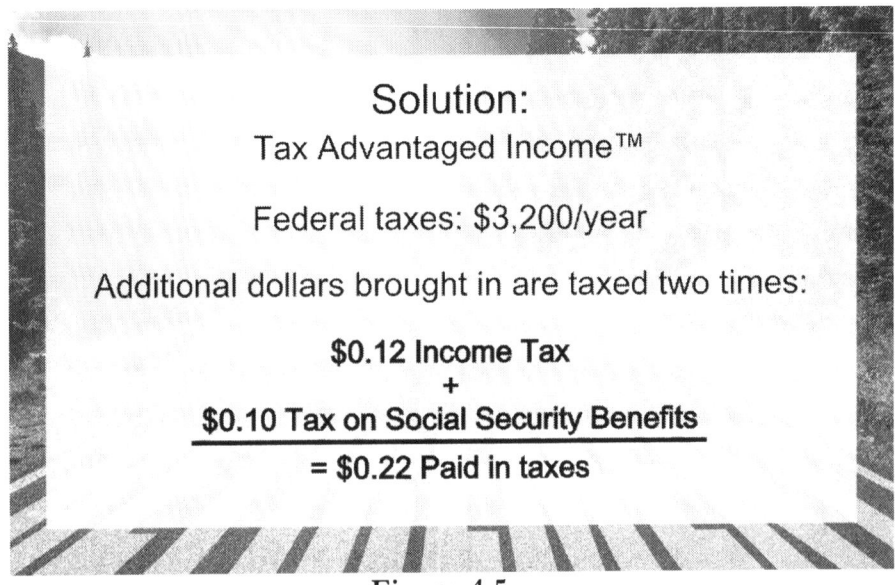

Figure 4.5

So, let's look at Don and Joan's situation after implementing their Tax Advantaged Income Plan. Look at Figure 4.5. With Tax-Advantaged Income, Don and Joan's total taxes would drop to about $3,200 a year."

"Holy cow!" Dick exclaimed, "Weren't they paying over $10,000 a year before?" Tommy nodded yes. Dick was now getting excited. "That's an unbelievable difference!"

Tommy smiled because he loved teaching this part: "Now, in their case, taxes on Social Security benefits weren't eliminated. However, they now only pay 12 cents of income tax on an extra dollar made and 10 cents of tax on their Social Security benefits. So if Don and Joan DID earn that one additional dollar of income, they would go from paying 41 cents of tax on that dollar down to 22 cents of tax.

Solution:
Tax Advantaged Income™

Compare	Before	After
Total Income	$133,200	$133,200
Federal Taxes	$10,474	$3,200

Amount of tax on extra dollar earned
$0.41 $0.22

BOTTOM-LINE SAVINGS:
$7,274 each year!

Figure 4.6

In figure 4.6, you can compare their previous and current situations. Their income stayed the same each month. The only difference is they are paying over $7,000 less in income taxes; and what excites me about saving on taxes is that it will typically be annual savings. So in their case, they're saving over $7,200 every single year."

"You're excited!" Dick shouted. "This is probably old hat for you. It's downright thrilling to me!" He said with a massive grin on his face. Jane couldn't resist smiling as well.

Tommy was smiling, too. "While our guest is here, we should have him cover one more topic."

"Oh, I don't mind if we skip it," Evil Uncle Sam quickly shot back.

Tommy would not have any of his attitude, "Sam, enough with the delays. Get on with the last topic so we can get rid of you."

• • •

Part 2: Protect Yourself From the Huge Tax Risk Most Are Ignoring

Evil Uncle Sam was perturbed by Tommy sharing how to avoid unnecessary taxes, but he couldn't help but become excited again to talk about another tax problem he was causing so many baby boomers.

"Alright," he began, "I must admit this one is pretty genius. You've probably heard it time and time again throughout your life. Think about it for a minute: have you ever been told that you should defer your taxes while you're working? The idea is that you are making more money now than you will in retirement, so avoid the taxes now and pay them later.

You may have heard something like that around tax time or when signing up for your company's 401k. It may have been on the news or at the office water cooler, or maybe even at a dinner party. Have you ever heard anything like that before?"

Dick nodded in agreement. "Oh, sure. I think everyone has heard that, and it makes sense. Like you said, you're obviously making more money when you're working than when you are retired. So, of course, you would want to defer your taxes."

Evil Uncle Sam was beaming. "Exactly! This idea has become so common that many baby boomers are approaching retirement with most or even all of their nest egg in their 401k or IRA or any other kind of tax-deferred account. Isn't that amazing?"

Jane looked at Dick and Tommy, "Uh oh. I'm guessing we're getting to the bad news."

Evil Uncle Sam continued, "It's not bad for me - it's great news for me! I touched on it a little earlier, but the problem for you and many others about to retire is that our debt as a country has exploded over the last couple of decades. Back in 2000, our total debt was $5.6 trillion. Now, it's over $33 trillion! [7]

And before this gets political - let's be honest: both parties love to spend! The debt goes up no matter who is in charge. The spending has been crazy and shows no signs of changing!"

Dick gave his best eye roll. "Don't get me started on politicians and spending. It makes my blood boil!"

Evil Uncle Sam couldn't contain himself. "Right? Their spending is incredible! Anyway, it excites me because every single economist and expert on finance agrees that eventually, there is only one possible solution to our debt problem: to raise taxes. Instead of withdrawing money to support your retirement and paying 12 or 22 percent in taxes, just imagine paying 30 or 40 percent. That may sound crazy, but it is a very real possibility."

Evil Uncle Sam paused for effect. Then, with a broad smile, he said, "So let me summarize that for you: our country's debt is so bad that everyone agrees that tax rates have to go up, and baby boomers have been doing what they were always told: to defer all of their taxes until retirement. Isn't that amazing?"

Dick and Jane were now both upset. Jane responded, "Oh my goodness. All that money in our IRAs could get taxed into oblivion."

Evil Uncle Same replied, "YES! Exactly!"

Tommy felt it was time to step in. "I think that explains the bad news pretty well. We can move to the good news, and if we're going there, we no longer don't need our repulsive guest over here. How does it sound if we get rid of him?"

"With pleasure!" Dick replied with excitement. While answering, he got out of his chair as if he would confront Evil Uncle Sam.

"Wait a second! Wait just a second!" Evil Uncle Sam said as he jumped out of his chair and backed away from the table. "I'll go. I promise I'll go. I have one last thing to say." Tommy groaned in anticipation of what he was about to hear.

Evil Uncle Sam smiled the most sinister smile he could while rubbing his hands together. He said, "Just remember, I'm here to take as much of your money as I can. Why? Because I loooove to spend money! And don't forget, I have the power to tax you, and you know I will! Hahaha!" His laugh was just as sinister as his smile.

Tommy intervened. "Alright, Sam. I can't take any more of your excitement. Why don't you see yourself out."

Dick couldn't agree more. "Thank you! Enough of this guy!" And just like that, Sam was gone.

Tommy started his lesson. "Alright, let's start with author David McKnight, who uses an example of the Road Runner in his best-selling book, "The Power of Zero."

"What possible application could a Road Runner episode have to my financial life? Well, as Americans who have grown accustomed to investing in tax-deferred accounts such as 401(k)s and IRAs, we find ourselves standing on the tracks with a very real train bearing down on us, and it's coming in the form of higher taxes. Now, given this reality, we have a couple of options. We can pretend like the problem doesn't exist and simply pull down the window shade. Or, we can implement some proven strategies that can help remove us from the train tracks."[3]

The good news is that the solution to this problem is reasonably straightforward, and SuperRetirementPlanner can help you figure out what's best for you. The first step is to see where you stand right now, which means understanding how your savings and investments are taxed. There are three possible ways they can be taxed:

1) Tax-deferred: as Sam mentioned, this is anything that hasn't been taxed yet. These types of accounts are how most Americans save for retirement. The most common are the 401k or a traditional IRA.

2) Taxable: this is anything where you pay taxes on it every year. It could be something like a bank CD or maybe an investment or brokerage account.

3) Tax-free: this is something that allows you to withdraw out of it without paying any taxes. The most common would be a Roth IRA or a Roth 401k.

So, in its simplest terms, if you have a significant portion of your nest egg in tax-deferred accounts, the solution is to have a strategy for shifting those funds out of tax-deferred and most likely into something tax-free." Tommy paused.

Dick responded, "Well, that sounds simple enough."

Tommy agreed, "Yes, the basics are simple, but the details are complicated. For example, when you claim your Social Security benefits affects this planning. Also, when you reach age 73, there are rules about how much you must take out of many of your retirement accounts. Those are called RMDs or Required Minimum Distributions. Those affect this planning as well.

That's where SuperRetirementPlanner comes in. He and his team will examine your situation and help you determine how much to do and when.

His team has shown me projections showing how this type of planning can easily save a family hundreds of thousands of dollars in taxes over their lifetime! I'm guessing you would like to see if the same is true for you.

"Without a doubt," Dick nodded. "I don't want to give that guy a penny more than I have to!"

"That was just the response I expected," Tommy said. "Look, it's late, and you've had a long day. I know you're probably eager to hear from the rest of the retirement villains, but let's stop here and pick up bright and early tomorrow."

This time Jane beat Dick to the punch. "I agree. As much as I would like to do all of this in one day, it's just too much. We'll see you tomorrow at sunrise!"

END NOTES

1. Tax Foundation, Tax Freedom Day and Tax Burden, April, 2019, taxfoundation.org/blog/tax-freedom-day-2019/
2. Congressional Budget Office, February 2023, www.cbo.gov/publication/58946
3. www.taxpolicycenter.org/fiscal-fact/highest-marginal-income-tax-rate-1913-2023
4. www.investopedia.com/ask/answers/013015/how-can-i-avoid-paying-taxes-my-social-security-income.asp
5. All calculations done through www.RetirementAnalyzer.com
6. www.irs.gov/pub/irs-pdf/f1040es.pdf
7. www.usdebtclock.org

Chapter 5

The Skyrocketing Cost of Healthcare

"The baby boomers' later life is going to be longer and more expensive than that of any previous generation."

Craig Garber, *The Retirement Myth*

Dick and Jane headed straight home. It had been a long and exhausting day. They drove most of the way in silence. Dick was ashamed and embarrassed. As the man of the house, he felt he should have been able to do all the retirement planning himself.

Finally, he broke the silence, "Honey, I'm so sorry. I figured I could do the whole plan myself. I had absolutely no idea how complicated a retirement plan could be!"

Jane had been furious when she had first heard that Dick hadn't shared Tommy's warnings. But as the day passed, she realized that Dick's intentions were good all along. "Darling, that's so sweet of you. I was mad at you before, but I understand you felt pressured to provide for us. Not only while you're working but also in retirement, and I realize that you wanted to get it all right. I really do understand."

Dick was relieved. The last thing he wanted to do was harm his beautiful wife of 36 years.

"But…" she continued, "You DO know how much we need SuperFinancialPlanner now…right?"

Dick quickly nodded, "Believe me, honey, I get it. We've only met three of these crazy villains, and yes, I definitely get it!" He smiled at his wife as he pulled into the driveway. After he parked the car, they shared a long embrace. Even with all the bad news shared by the retirement villains, they felt like they knew how to put together a successful retirement plan for the first time in their lives. It was a liberating feeling!

That night, Dick and Jane fell fast asleep within seconds of their heads hitting their pillows. It wasn't just the exhaustion of the day – it was also the peaceful feeling of getting on track with their plan. After they'd been sleeping a while, there was a sudden cloud of smoke at the end of the bed. When the smoke cleared, a woman appeared. She wore a nurse's uniform and held a pile of medical bills in her left hand.

Dick and Jane had never been more startled. They were shocked and disoriented. At the end of the bed stood their guest – she greeted them with a belly laugh.

"Did I surprise you?" She somehow managed to ask as she continued laughing.

"Oh my goodness, you're a retirement villain, aren't you?!" Dick exclaimed, "You could have given me a heart attack!"

At this, the woman laughed even harder. "That's hilarious, especially considering who I am!"

"So you ARE a retirement villain?" Dick asked, "This is crazy. It's like *A Christmas Carol* or something! I hope we won't be visited by two more ghosts tonight – at some point, I will need some sleep!"

The woman said, "Very funny. But I can assure you that I am NOT a ghost. I am real and one of the nastiest retirement villains in existence, if I do say so myself."

By this time, Dick and Jane had calmed down. They had met three other retirement villains just that day. Once the shock of being awoken by someone at the end of the bed had subsided, they realized they were just back on the same ride they were on earlier in the day.

Jane joined the conversation: "Okay, we give, who are you?"

"I thought you'd never ask!" The woman responded – with a smile, of course. "My name is Sarah Self-Pay. It is such a pleasure to meet you!"

"Sarah Self-Pay?" Dick and Jane said simultaneously and looked at each other. Dick continued, "What in the world does that mean?"

"I am the retirement villain of health care," Sarah Self-Pay responded, "You see, having medical problems is bad enough, but when you have to pay astronomical amounts for your healthcare, that just adds insult to injury. Literally. Get it?" She belly laughed at her own joke.

Jane heard what Sarah Self-Pay said but was still confused: "Okay, I guess that makes some sense. But we have health insurance, and when we retire, we'll have Medicare, so aren't we pretty much taken care of when it comes to this stuff?"

Sarah Self-Pay began to laugh even harder, "Oh, that's always the funniest thing everyone says! So you have no idea, do you? It sounds to me like I need to give you the whole story. Are you ready?"

Dick and Jane nodded yes. "Okay," Sarah Self-Pay began, "I promise I won't skip a thing – because I just LOVE sharing bad news! Let's see…where to begin. How about here:

For your retirement plan to be effective, it must consider the issues that are currently having the most significant financial impact on retirees. Few would argue that the cost of disability and long-term care is one of the biggest. Some say it has become the greatest financial threat to middle-class and upper-middle-class Americans today.

In 2001, the National Endowment for Financial Education sponsored a two-day symposium in Scottsdale, Arizona, to study one of the most critical issues retirees face. The underlying theme throughout the report generated from this "think tank" was that long-term care could become a national crisis.[1] Fast forward many years later, and we have overwhelming evidence of the problem, as more than eight million Americans need some form of long-term care.[2]

"Oh my!" Jane interjected, "That's a scary statistic!"

As difficult as it was to imagine, Sarah Self-Pay's smile grew, "Oh, don't worry. I've got plenty more bad news!

As I'm sure Lady Longevity covered with you, Americans are living longer than ever before. As the population ages, we can expect that the need for long-term care will increase proportionately. The Baby Boomers are aging – the first of 79 million of them turned 65 in 2011.[3]

According to US Census projections, during the next 20 years, the number of Americans age 65 will increase by 76 percent. By 2030, one in five Americans will be a senior citizen![4] With an aging population facing increased healthcare needs and rising care costs, and many with no insurance coverage to pay for it, we certainly could have a long-term care crisis of epic proportions.

There wasn't much talk of nursing homes and assisted living facilities back in the '70s. But from 1970 to 1990, nursing home expenditures in the United States increased faster than any other healthcare cost, with a 12.7 percent annual growth rate.[5]

Another contributing factor to this potential crisis is that medical advancements and improvements in health care now help us survive things like heart attacks and strokes that were more likely to kill us years ago. Medical technology has produced new drugs, diagnostic equipment, and cutting-edge surgeries that add years to the average life expectancy of retirees. So, an advanced healthcare system is keeping seniors alive well into their 80s and 90s, often well past their projected life expectancy.

The average stay in a nursing home varies with a person's illness, medical condition, and general state of health. The longer we live, the more susceptible we become to other illnesses that typically affect the aged, such as Alzheimer's disease, vascular dementia, and severe mobility problems. Clearly, this increases the demand for nursing homes and assisted living facilities. These conditions, like many that affect the elderly, don't respond well to medications and surgeries and aren't easily or successfully treated or cured.

Instead, as these illnesses progress, they often lead to a need for custodial care – and lead the aging senior down the path to the poorhouse trying to pay for that care. As the Invisible Enemy should have told you, the average cost of a nursing home stay is $95,000 per year! And these costs have been rising for years. That is a retirement expense that most never contemplated, and their nest eggs could never take that kind of a hit.

Another reason this has become such a big crisis is the geographic expansion of the American family. It wasn't that long ago when most children stayed close to home. Now, instead of moving down the road or across town, many adult children are moving across the state, country, or even overseas. Regardless of whether they're moving by choice or out of need to look for work, this is a game changer for the family's health care.

When an elderly parent or grandparent became ill, it was easier for children and grandchildren to help with care and keep their disabled family member at home. One by one, families have become separated – spread out across the country – and are no longer as easily able to help when dad has a stroke or mom falls and breaks her hip. This shift in the modern-day family is just one of the many dynamics that have led us to where we are today: with a potential long-term care crisis.

Government programs like Medicare and Medicaid were not initially designed to handle the number of retirees who need care today. And as you will see, Medicare turns its back on retirees in their greatest time of need and doesn't care about long-term care. Without any help from government or private insurance, how long your money last if you get stuck with a monthly bill of $8,000 or more? How many retirees could afford that bill? More and more aging retirees face declining health, rising life expectancy, and an increased need for health care with no way to pay for it."

"That is awful!" Jane said. "You said something about Medicare not helping us as much as we expect. What do you mean by that?"

MEDICARE – THE VANISHING GOVERNMENT BENEFIT

"Ah, great question!" Sarah Self-Pay always enjoyed some participation. It let her know she was scaring her listeners – which brought her great joy. "I like to call Medicare the Vanishing Government Benefit! Here's why:

Despite the rapidly increasing cost and need for long-term care services, most retirees and their families are still shocked to learn that Medicare doesn't pay for nursing home or assisted living costs. They mistakenly believe Medicare will take care of all of their medical expenses. Unfortunately, this false sense of security contributes to inaction – the failure to plan – which can be financially devastating when a disability strikes. The reality is Medicare doesn't care about long-term care.

It's easy to see why Medicare and Medicaid will do whatever it takes to avoid paying for your nursing care. The extent of the federal government's long-term liabilities and commitments to programs such as Medicare and Medicaid is not well known among the general public. These commitments have risen from just over $20 trillion in 2000 to $75.9 trillion in 2022.[6]

Most are stunned when they learn how little Medicare will pay for nursing care. First, Medicare coverage for nursing care has a maximum of 100 days. Second, Medicare could cover the first 20 days but then requires you to pay the first $130 per day until day 100.[7] Finally, during those 100 days, Medicare will cover skilled care but not custodial care.

Custodial care essentially includes assistance with basic activities of daily living, like walking, transferring, toileting, eating, bathing, and grooming. When retirees are most vulnerable, and need the most care, our health system often leaves them with few options.

What happened to John F. Kennedy's vision for universal medical insurance for all aged Americans?[8] The Medicare program was supposed to be there for all retirees regardless of their healthcare needs. Instead, it has shrunk to exclude those afflicted with some of the most devastating illnesses – even though they most likely paid into the Medicare system since its inception.

It doesn't make sense, but it's true. Medicare pays if you need heart surgery, chemotherapy, or a hip replacement. If you have Alzheimer's disease, severe dementia, or are completely bedridden, Medicare does not pay. It's like the diagnosis lottery, where certain illnesses are covered, and others are not. How is that fair?"

Dick was furious now. "That's ridiculous! Why in the world would our government favor some illnesses over others?!"

"Yes, that's it exactly!" Sarah Self-Pay responded, "I'm so glad you can see. I've made quite a mess for retirees, haven't I? So anyway, the bottom line is: If you can't get better, Medicare won't help you.

Let's consider many of the different healthcare situations you could find yourself in, and we'll look at how or if the various government programs will assist you. We start with the healthy, vigorous retiree. She may still be working or have recently retired and is active in family or community life. She may take some medication and may eventually develop chronic health problems like diabetes or heart disease. She may face hospitalizations or surgeries and may ultimately have declining health with mobility issues.

Throughout this stage of her health care, Medicare does an excellent job of paying many of the bills, and supplemental health insurance often helps as well.

The following example is a perfect illustration: If you've ever had trouble sleeping, you may have seen one of those late-night ads for the Scooter Store. These commercials are compelling because they essentially say, "If we can't get Medicare or your insurance to cover the cost of your scooter …. We'll give it to you for free!"

Isn't that amazing? They have to be confident that Medicare will pay for these scooters, or they could never make that kind of an offer on television. They'd go broke if they did! But they know that Medicare does a great job paying for active retirees with mobility problems, so they can afford to make those claims.

And with that kind of commitment by Medicare, it's easy for retirees to get comfortable thinking that Medicare will pay all their long-term care bills. So where do all the problems start? Right when you step over into the next stage of health. Because if your mobility issues worsen to the point where you need some in-home assistance, which can cost $15-$25 per hour, Medicare no longer covers you.

Maybe you live alone, or your spouse is frail and can't lift you, and you need to hire someone to come to your home and help you get out of bed, or help you bathe or get dressed, or check your insulin levels, or stay with you for an hour so your spouse can have a little break. Medicare doesn't cover these situations. They aren't paying anymore; you have to pay for that yourself. I wonder what JFK would think of that?

And what happens when you go further along, and your health declines, and it's not safe for you to stay in your own home anymore? Maybe you need to move to an assisted living facility where there are no stairs, and you can get more care in a safe environment with people to monitor and check on you. Ensure you eat, take your medicines on time, and don't wander away. Well, Medicare doesn't cover that, either. The cost at this stage can be $2,000 to $5,000 per month, depending on how much assistance you need.

What becomes of the fragile senior whose health care needs require 24-hour care? What if your spouse has advanced Alzheimer's or dementia and must be monitored at all times? Or what if your spouse is bedridden and can no longer communicate? Does Medicare cover your nursing home bill, which, on average, costs about $8,000 every month? You guessed it – not at all.

Although another government program called Medicaid may assist you with your nursing home bills, you won't get any help until you have spent most of your money first. That's right – the government will force you to spend so much of your own money that by the time help arrives, you may be left with almost nothing, despite the fact that you've paid taxes and Social Security all these years. Unless you have a plan, the government has a plan for you – spend down your life savings, and then we will help you!"

Dick was losing his temper. "I don't know how much more of this I can take!"

Jane gently placed her hand on Dick's shoulder. "I know it's hard, but we need to hear it."

"You need to hear it, and I love talking about it!" Sarah Self-Pay said – way too happily for Dick's taste. But he let her continue.

"So where can you turn for help when Medicare doesn't cover you? Many turn to Medicaid, a government program designed to pay the health care expenses of the impoverished. That's right, when your government health insurance plan (Medi*care*) doesn't cover you, the next available option is Medi*caid*, which won't help you at all until you spend down your nest egg.

Listen to this painfully accurate quote from Robert L. Kane, Professor of Long-Term Care and Aging at the University of Minnesota School of Public Health: "We have facetiously described the American approach to paying for long-term care as universal coverage with a deductible equal to all your assets and a co-payment equal to all your income."[9] That is not a pretty picture, is it?

Medicaid is misunderstood on many counts. Because of the similarity in names, it is often confused with Medicare. Medicaid provides financial assistance to retirees to pay for nursing home costs and a limited amount of home health care. The largest share of nursing home residents – currently about 59% – pay their skilled nursing home bill with money from Medicaid.[10]

While Medicaid is a federal program, it is administered by each state, often with conflicting, confusing, and inconsistent results. The National Academy of Elder Law Attorneys has referred to Medicaid as one of the most complex laws in the United States.[11] Rules vary widely from state to state.

Dick was depressed. "Okay, I admit that listening to the other retirement villains was bad, but none were as painful as this!"

Sarah Self-Pay jumped up with excitement. "Oh, thank you! You just made my day! And here's one more piece of depressing news I can't wait to share with you: pretty much anything you own is considered available for what is often referred to as the Medicaid spend down – and you will be expected to use it. All your CDs, money market accounts, retirement accounts, stocks, bonds, most annuities, and any other 'nest egg' type of accounts will be considered countable resources that can disqualify you from Medicaid benefits unless they are spent down."

At this point, Sarah Self-Pay stopped. Her smile seemed to get bigger and bigger as the conversation passed. Now, it was as if her smile was as big as her face.

"Well, we need to do something about this," Jane blurted out.

Dick nodded, "That's a good point. If we've learned one thing in the past day, it's that there are tons of problems out there, but there are solutions, too. So what can we do to protect ourselves?"

Sarah Self-Pay laughed yet again, "Why in the world would I have any interest in telling you about that?" she asked with a devilish grin.

"Look honey," Jane said to Dick, "There's sunlight coming through the blinds. It's morning already. Why don't you call Tommy and invite him over for breakfast?!"

Dick smiled. "That's a terrific idea. I'll call him after I do one other thing."

"What's that?" Jane wondered.

"First, I have to tell our villain friend here to get lost!" Dick said with his own devilish smile on his face. He sensed that the retirement villains could not stay whenever told to leave. At that instant, Sarah Self-Pay gasped and was taken away in a cloud of smoke.

Jane gave her husband a big hug. "You're certainly getting the hang of this."

Dick smiled. "I better call Tommy!"

"Wow, that was delicious!" Tommy exclaimed after putting down three eggs, two pieces of bacon, and three buttermilk pancakes. "Brenda's been visiting her family for almost a week now, and you know that means I've been eating cereal for breakfast each day since!" Dick and Jane understood and smiled.

"Okay, let's get back to work," Tommy said, "Sarah Self-Pay paid you a visit. She covered all the horrible news about health care costs in retirement, right?" Dick and Jane nodded yes. "Okay, good. At least I get to tell you that there are some things you can do.

A few strategies that can help you save money and avoid becoming impoverished, even if you are facing an immediate nursing home crisis and have been told you must spend down your life savings. The clock is ticking, and NOW is the best time to devise and implement your game plan.

There isn't any one perfect solution, but there are six most commonly used options:

1) Use your own assets. You can use your cash, stocks, IRAs, home, etc., to pay for a nursing home stay.

Using your assets is the default plan. I would call it 'self-insuring.' Of course, the advantage to this option is that you're not paying any insurance premiums, and hopefully, equally obvious is the disadvantage: that all of your hard-earned money is still at risk.

Jane squished her nose in disapproval. "Okay, I'm ready to hear about the other options!"

Tommy smiled. "I completely agree!

2) Transfer assets out of your estate more than five years before anyone applies for Medicaid, and then let Medicaid pay.

The second option is transferring your assets out of your name at least five years before needing care. The obvious problem with this option is that no one knows when they will need nursing care! Also, if you've done a decent job of saving, transferring your assets away would be quite challenging!

3) Buy long-term care insurance.

Buying long-term care insurance used to look like a great option. You would buy enough insurance to cover the risk of going into a nursing home, just like you buy auto insurance to cover the risk of getting into an accident.

However, this industry has gone through a massive transformation over the last ten years. Many companies have left the industry because the claims were far more expensive than the insurance companies expected.

And now, many retirees who still have policies face frequent premium increases from their insurance carriers. Yes, that's right:

the biggest problem with long-term care insurance is that the company can raise your rates, which is the last thing you want to have happen when you're retired and living on a fixed income!"

"Great," Dick grouses, "First, I'm worried about a nursing home getting all our hard-earned money. Then, I'm mad about the government not helping to pay for it, and after that, the insurance company makes me even more upset by jacking up my premiums! I'm thinking I'll take a hard pass on that option!"

Tommy nodded understandingly, "Dick, I get it. We made the same decision; this type of insurance is becoming far less popular, but there could be certain people that it fits.

Those who decide to buy it they need to be careful with long-term care insurance salespeople. They sometimes push you to add many features to your policy to raise your premium and increase their commission!

Obviously, you don't want your "advisor" working against you! This is another example of why you want someone you can trust instead of working with an insurance or financial salesperson. Instead, the best approach is usually to cover the most risk for the smallest possible premium. That usually means few or no bells and whistles.

4)   Invest in asset-based long-term care insurance.

For some retirees, asset-based long-term care insurance is the most appealing option. Here's how it works: you have to make an initial investment. Doing so ensures that you will never have to pay any monthly or annual premiums. Then, if you need nursing care at any time in the future, the policy pays for the care for you just like a traditional long-term care policy would. However, if you never need nursing care, your family is guaranteed to receive money back from the insurance company when you pass away. So, no matter what happens, you're guaranteed to get some kind of return on your money. Here's a quick example:

Take Doris: when she was 65, she invested $50,000 into asset based long term care. If she ever needs nursing care, she will have over $312,000 of care that can be paid for by her policy. In addition, if she never needs nursing care, her family will receive over $104,000 from the insurance company when she dies.

The biggest downside to this option is that the money you place into the policy is no longer invested or generating income for you to live off of. It's for this reason alone that many people make a different choice.

5) Buy life insurance with a long-term care rider.

The next option is a specific type of life insurance. As our worries about nursing care increased, life insurance companies came up with a pretty nifty idea: what if you could access the death benefit on your policy if you needed nursing care?

That's what a policy with a long-term care rider allows. So, if you die, the death benefit goes to your beneficiary, but if you need nursing care before dying, you can access the death benefit to help pay for your care.

On top of that, life insurance has a valuable benefit that long-term care insurance doesn't: the life insurance company cannot increase your premiums!

"Wow!" Dick exclaimed, "That sounds great! So what's the catch?"

Tommy responded, "Well, there's always a string attached, right? In this case, the most significant string attached is that the premiums are expensive. But the benefits can be considerable. So, this can be an excellent choice if the premiums fit your budget.

6) Invest in an annuity with a long-term care rider.

The last option on our list is allocating part of your nest egg toward a specific type of annuity. In this example, you place part of your nest egg into an annuity that will provide you with a lifetime income guarantee, and don't worry – if you're married, you can set up the income to last as long as both of you do.

That is pretty straightforward when it comes to annuities. The unique thing the rider provides is additional income if you need nursing care.

As a quick and easy example, let's say you have an annuity that will pay you $1,000 a month when you retire. If you ever need nursing care, the annuity will pay you double – in this case, $2,000 a month. Some in the industry call this a 'doubler.'

Now, you know that an extra $1,000 a month won't cover all of your costs of nursing care. But this is a way to help cover the expenses without buying an insurance policy." Tommy paused.

"Is that it?" Dick asked.

Tommy chuckled a little. "Yep, that's it."

"Hmmm…" Dick was pondering what he had just heard. "It sounds like there's not a simple solution to this problem."

"That's a great observation, Dick," Tommy said, "It depends on each person's situation, and that's why working with a professional is so important."

"Point taken, and I couldn't agree more!" Dick said. "Alright, we're up; we've had a great breakfast. Why not keep going?"

"I couldn't agree more!" Tommy said with a wink and a smile. "It's a beautiful day outside. Why don't we head out by your pool?"

This question made Jane smile. "Tommy, do you think we should go out by the pool because the weather is so nice? Or is there some other reason?"

Tommy was definitely enjoying himself. "Don't you wish you knew?" Jane would have to wait just a little longer to learn the answer to her question.

END NOTES

1. LONG TERM CARE: Our Next National Crisis? A Think Tank Sponsored by the National Endowment for Financial Education, Scottsdale, Arizona – May 6-8, 2000.
2. https://caregiver.org/selected-long-term-care-statistics
3. How Will Baby Boomers' Retirement Affect Stocks?, *USA Today*, 7/19/2010
4. Elder Boom Will Be Felt Worldwide, *US News & World Report*, 7/20/2009
5. Containing US health care costs: what bullet to bite? – Cost Containment Issues, Methods and Experiences. Health Care Financing Review, Annual 1991 by Stephen F. Jencks, George J. Schreiber.
6. "The Government's Financial Position and Condition," https://www.fiscal.treasury.gov/reports-statements/financial-report/government-financial-position-and-condition.html
7. "Medicare Coverage of Skilled Nursing Facility Care," December 2022, https://www.medicare.gov/Pubs/pdf/10153-Medicare-Skilled-Nursing-Facility-Care.pdf
8. Lyndon B. Johnson is credited with ultimately passing the Medicare bill into law in 1965. In fact, Medicare was the brainchild of John F. Kennedy, and was the focal point of his campaign. President Kennedy began the fight for Medicare in 1961, yet after an 18 month battle was unable to drum up the necessary support in the Senate, where his Medicare bill was defeated 52-48, due to vehement opposition by the AMA. *Health Care Reform: Revising the Medicare Story, POLICY AND MEDICINE, 12/1/2008*
9. *The Retirement Myth*, Craig S. Karpel
10. "Principles for Assessing Medicaid Nursing Facility Payment Policies," March 2023, https://www.macpac.gov/wp-

content/uploads/2023/03/Chapter-2-Principles-for-Assessing-Medicaid-Nursing-Facility-Payment-Policies.pdf
11. Medicaid: The Issue, www.naela.org/Public/About_NAELA/Public_or_Consumer/Medicaid.aspx, NAELA 2008.
12. P.L. 109-171 Sec. 6011, 6014 (D

Chapter 6

Wall Street Greed

"Fortunes are made on Wall Street by catering to your greed. Not a penny is to be made protecting you from Wall Street's greed. That's your job."

Wall Street Versus America: The Rampant Greed and Dishonesty That Imperil Your Investments, by Gary Weiss

Tommy, Dick, and Jane made their way straight to the pool in the backyard. It wasn't an elaborate setup, but gave Dick and Jane all they wanted behind their home: a place to relax, entertain friends, and beat the heat of the notoriously hot Metropolis summer days.

On the way to the pool, Dick and Jane whispered back and forth, which made Tommy smile even more.

"Okay, Tommy," Dick said as they all slid into their patio furniture beside the pool, "Jane and I are dying to know. The next retirement villain must have something to do with the pool. Do they like to swim? I hope it's not a piranha!"

Tommy laughed, "Sit down and relax. It's not a piranha. It sounds like you're ready to keep moving. You were right that the pool is involved. But it's not that he likes the water. It's because he needs the water."

At that moment, a cloud of smoke appeared at the pool's edge at the water's surface. This time, in addition to the cloud of smoke, Dick and Jane noticed a very cool breeze. When the smoke faded away, Dick and Jane could see nasty-looking man with an icy glare, white and blue tights, and a cape…almost like a superhero. His hair looked like solid ice, and he held a large gray freeze gun.

"I'm not sure who this villain is," said Dick, "But if you always bring that cool breeze with you, you can stop by any time!"

Tommy frowned at Dick's comment. "I hope you enjoy the laughs while you can, Dick, because this retirement villain could decimate your portfolio if you allow him to."

"Thanks, Tommy!" The ice man bellowed, "It's nice when people give credit where credit is due for a change!"

Dick was confused. "What are you, made of ice? What in the world does that have to do with our retirement?"

"Good observation," Tommy calmly answered, "Forgive me for not making a proper introduction. Dick and Jane, this is Iceberg Ivan. So, yes, he is made of ice. But he doesn't represent the cold or freezing. He got his name because of icebergs."

Dick was still confused. "Okay, so he could sink our retirement like the Titanic?"

"Let me clear this up, Tommy!" Iceberg Ivan quickly said, "You see, Dick, I think it's safe to say you know what a regular chunk of ice is. But an iceberg is a unique type of chunk of ice. The difference is important because an iceberg is far more than what meets the eye. In fact, according to www.Wikipedia.com, a typical iceberg only has 1/9th of its volume above the surface. So the point I'm trying to get to is I'm a lot more dangerous to you than you realize!"

Jane was quickly getting the point. "Okay, that makes sense. But how exactly do you hurt our retirement? It's not by cooling down the water in our pool!"

"Well said, Jane," Tommy replied. "Iceberg Ivan represents fees on your nest egg. These fees and costs can take on all sorts of names and appearances: account fees, maintenance fees, management fees, wrap account fees, advisory fees, early withdrawal penalties, surrender charges, and the list goes on and on."

Dick and Jane nodded in agreement. At one point or another, since they started saving for their retirement, they had paid many of the types of fees that Tommy listed. "Okay," Jane said, "I've got my notepad and pen ready. I think we're ready to hear all about Ivan and these fees."

Iceberg Ivan looked over at Tommy, who nodded back at him. "Very well," said Ivan, "I'm pretty sure you're not going to enjoy this as much as I will!"

...

While Ivan lived off of hiding most of his fees, he couldn't help but savor the chance to explain just how badly all those fees can hurt retirees: "I'm sure you understand that companies that hold your savings and investments are going to charge you fees since that's the business that they're in. Some fees are just little annoyances, but we will focus on the fees that can truly eat into your nest egg slowly and silently. They are far more significant and dangerous than originally meet the eye."

"Like icebergs!" Jane interjected.

Ivan always enjoyed it when his listeners were getting the symbolism he represented. "Very good! These types of fees are almost always being charged on investment accounts. While fees affect practically every type of account, the mutual fund industry represents much of what goes on at Wall Street. So, let's focus our attention there.

Now, the original idea of a mutual fund was a good one. Rather than forcing someone to pick a stock to invest in, the idea of a mutual fund allowed you to invest a little bit into many different stocks. In concept, this is a great idea. It allows you to invest smaller amounts of money and reduce your risk of losing a lot if something goes wrong with one stock."

"Sounds good so far," Jane said, knowing Ivan had only shared part of the story.

Dick chuckled, "Yeah, it always starts that way, doesn't it."

Iceberg Ivan continued, "Over time, mutual funds became increasingly popular, and the money poured in. For example, in 1998, total assets were about $5.5 trillion. By 2021, that number was just shy of $27 trillion." [1]

Dick questioned, "Wait, is that trillion with a 't?'" Ivan nodded that he was correct. "Wow, those are some crazy numbers."

Tommy knew this was where he needed to jump in. "Ivan, I need to speak my peace here because I get angry. Typically, when a product becomes popular, more companies join the market. This creates competition, and it drives prices down. But in the case of mutual funds, the exact opposite happened. Fees actually went up. Ivan, why don't you tell them a little about how Wall Street gets away with all of this?"

Ivan's smile quickly faded. After glaring at Tommy for just longer than necessary, he turned to Dick and Jane and said, "Something told me you would make me do that. Alright, here's how they do it:

The easiest way to explain this is with quotes from some of the most respected people studying investment fees. For example, as Gregory Baer and Gary Gensler wrote in their book, *"The Great Mutual Fund Trap"*:

> *"There's a reason you don't consider the costs of investing, of course. Mutual funds and brokers have constructed a system where the costs are practically invisible."*

As much as I hate to admit this, Baer and Gensler are absolutely correct. Most investments have found ways to make fees practically invisible. I say practically invisible because those fees typically must be disclosed in a prospectus. The problem is that these are miles long and written by Philadelphia lawyers. I suspect people read them about as often as the privacy notice updates you receive from your cell phone provider. Let me ask, have you ever read that from beginning to end?"

Dick was already angry, and now his face was turning red. "Oh, come on! You know they write those things and give it to you in the tiniest print to ensure that no one reads it!"

Iceberg Ivan flashed a knowing smile. "I won't disagree with that. With many Wall Street accounts, your fees are taken out of your account over the course of the year, and you never see it on your statement."

"He's right," Jane interrupted, "I've tried to look at our statements before, and they never say what we're paying. I knew there was no way they were working for free."

"Oh, that's a good one!" Iceberg Ivan exclaimed with a hearty laugh, "No, they certainly aren't working for free, and listen to this: when people around Wall Street talk about mutual fund management fees, they often toss around a figure like 1% per year. Yet, many studies show that a better estimate of the total cost is 3.1% per year. I believe that Richard Rutner summarizes it best in his book, *"The Trouble with Mutual Funds:"*

> *"Expense ratios average 1.6% per year, sales charges 0.5%, turnover generated portfolio transactions costs 0.7%, and opportunity costs-when funds hold cash rather than remain fully invested in stocks-0.3%. The average mutual fund investor loses 3.1% of his investment returns to these costs each year."*

Dick was quickly losing his temper. "Wait a minute! Are you telling me that my investment company has been making over 3% a year off of me, and they don't even have to show it on my statement? My retirement account is about $500,000. 3% of $500,000 is $15,000 a year. That should be illegal!"

"Hold on there, Dick," Iceberg Ivan responded, "Your company may not charge you that much. That's just the average. Your company may be charging you much less!"

"OR they may be charging you much more!" Tommy said. He wasn't going to let Ivan leave out part of the truth! "And don't forget what we learned from Lady Longevity. If your retirement lasts 30 years, that $15,000 a year would total $450,000 in fees - just during your retirement!"

"I feel sick," Dick said, "You're right: $15,000 a year is chump change compared to costing me hundreds of thousands of dollars!"

Tommy nodded. "Believe me, Dick, I was just as shocked as you. Ivan read to Dick and Jane some of the quotes from experts urging people to move away from these types of high-fee investments."

"Awww, you're no fun!" Iceberg Ivan replied. "Okay, here are a few of the ones Tommy always wants me to include. Let's start with best-selling author Ric Edelman from his book, *The Lies About Money:*"

> *"There's no greater pitfall than the one created by the mutual fund industry. There's no other way to say it: The industry is ripping you off. You are incurring greater risks, lower returns, and higher fees than you realize, and as a result, you are in danger of not achieving your financial goals.*
>
> *The situation is shocking — and no one is more astonished than me. My firm, one of the largest and best-known investment advisory firms in the nation, has placed $4 billion of our clients' assets into mutual funds. I've been the mutual fund industry's biggest proponent.*
>
> *No longer. Jean and I have now sold all our investments in mutual funds. All my colleagues at Edelman Financial have done likewise, and our clients are following our advice. You need to sell all your mutual funds too.*

Excuse me for being blunt, but the fact is that the mutual fund industry is now flush with liars, crooks, and charlatans. Daily business activities include deceit, hidden costs, undisclosed risks, deceptive trade practices, conflicts of interest, and fundamental violations of trust – all at your expense.

No wonder that the highly regarded David Swensen, chief investment officer of Yale University's $15 billion endowment fund, wrote in Unconventional Success: A Fundamental Approach to Personal Investment that there is "overwhelming evidence that proves the failure of the mutual fund industry."

Mr. Swensen is right. The industry's ethical breaches are not only insulting to us as investors, but they have caused you and me real economic losses. ...I no longer tolerate the situation. We've sold all our holdings of mutual funds. You should too."

"Speaking of David Swensen," Iceberg Ivan continued, "He has been considered by many to be one of the most successful portfolio managers of the last 40 years. Here are a few more of his comments from his book *"Unconventional Success:"*

"The failure of the mutual fund industry to produce attractive investment results stems from the inherent conflict between behaving as a fiduciary and acting as a profit-maximizer. The contest between serving investor interests and making money never even makes the starting gate. Profits win in a runaway.

Fees contribute substantially to the gap between investor aspirations and performance reality. The mutual fund industry levies an assorted collection of charges, including up-front loads, contingent deferred sales loads, standard management fees, distribution and marketing assessments and incentive payments. The aggregate of the compensation paid to mutual fund managers virtually guarantees that investors fail to achieve market-beating results.

In the final analysis, the benefits of active management accrue only to the mutual fund management companies, not to the investor. Asset managers profit, while investors lose."

"Here's another great quote," Ivan pushed on, "from author Gary Weiss in his book, *"Wall Street Versus America: The Rampant Greed and Dishonesty That Imperil Your Investments"*:

"Mutual fund companies cheerfully overcharge you for inflated fees and expenses, trade too much, pay through the nose in commissions, and overpay their pals in the brokerage industry in return for office space, research, and other perks, with you footing the bill. They are not neurotic or hesitant as they overcharge you. They confidently charge you fees that they don't deserve whether they are making or losing money, and they have job security that would make a postman envious.

The real mutual fund Scandals are straightforward. The real scandals involve Sunday school morality and simple concepts, such as "taking." The money is there, so they take."

Dick sighed: "This is all making me sick to my stomach. It feels pretty hopeless. I sure hope you'll tell us that SuperRetirementPlanner can help us with this."

"Oh, good grief!" Iceberg Ivan shouted, "The last thing I want to do is hear about that guy!"

Tommy couldn't help but smile. "Goodbye, Ivan! Now we're going to talk about how to fight you!"

As soon as Tommy finished talking, a cloud of smoke appeared at the edge of the pool, and when it had faded away, Ivan was gone.

Jane was ready for answers and had her pen and pad of paper ready for notes. "Okay, Tommy. Tell us what we can do to fight the iceberg!"

"Jane," Tommy responded, "I love your excitement; SuperRetirementPlanner can give you far more information and examples than I can. So, I'll let him cover most of it, but I can share one fundamental principle he has taught me and two additional tips.

...

The fundamental principle for considering any investment or account fee: what does this cost me, and what value am I receiving?

Another way to say this is how author Antti Ilmanen writes in his 2022 book, *Investing Amid Low Expected Returns*:

> *"Trading costs and asset management fees diminish investor performance. Yet, while cost consciousness is appropriate, the goal should be to maximize net returns adjusted for risk, and not to minimize costs or fees."*

You see, the problem with some mutual funds is that they invest your money in many of the same stocks in the S&P 500 but charge you all kinds of fees to do so. Imagine paying around 3% in fees when you could invest your money in an S&P 500 index fund for nearly nothing. Amazingly, there are now index funds with fees as low as 0.02%!"

Dick interrupted Tommy. "Wait, are there funds that do that?"

Tommy nodded, "Oh yes. Trillions of dollars in mutual funds are investing in the largest companies based in America. There's another name for those companies: the S&P 500!"

Dick shook his head, and Tommy continued. "So here's the deal: it has been proven time and time again that very few people want to manage their own nest egg throughout their retirement. There's just too much at stake. Think about times like 2008 and 2009 when the stock market dropped in half. Or during COVID in 2020. The market dropped by 33% in 33 days. There is just too much riding on our investments to toss them into an S&P 500 fund and hope for the best."

This time, Jane was nodding, "Nope. That is not something we would be comfortable with. I wouldn't be able to sleep at night."

"Exactly," Tommy agreed. "So, I'll quickly share some ways an investment can provide value for a fee. Again, I'm no expert. I'll let SuperRetirementPlanner give you the details.

Less Risk: Some investments are designed to lower the amount of risk you take if the stock market falls. If the investment can protect you from losing money, that could be worth quite a fee!

More Income: Some investments are designed to generate more income than others. That isn't important to most people until they're close to retirement; but once you're at retirement, it suddenly sounds exciting if an investment can give you 5, 6, 7, or 8% in income to help you cover your expenses. The key here is to make sure you know what the income is you would receive AFTER fees!

Access to Other Investments: Some investments are easy to invest in: U.S. stocks and bonds, for example. There are literally thousands of mutual funds offering these, but there are many other types of investments out there - many of which that could benefit retirees. Examples that come to mind would be private equity, private debt, private real estate portfolios, and real assets such as oil, gas, and timber."

Dick interrupted Tommy. "Wow, those sound interesting! Let's talk about those some more! Honey, keep that notepad handy!"

Jane rolled her eyes. Tommy chuckled, "I'm so sorry to get you excited, Dick. Those are topics for another time, but I promise we will get to them.

Before we stop, let me cover two other tips that SuperRetirementPlanner has taught me:

...

FIRST, ARE THE FEES HIDDEN, OR CAN YOU SEE THEM?

As we've discussed, the ability of Wall Street companies to hide fees is complicated and everywhere. It's always better if you're able to see the fees. For example, more and more financial advisors show the fee by charging a flat percentage on your account. That fee may be 1% or 2% a year, for example. It all depends on the chosen investments, how they're being managed, and often on whether you're receiving other services as well, such as income and tax planning.

Now let me warn you, it's not fun to actually SEE these fees! I just think you have to get used to it. It's better to know than to stick your head in the sand."

Jane was nodding again. "Yes, that makes total sense. Seeing 1% of $500,000 isn't fun, but it's certainly better than accepting hidden fees."

"Exactly," Tommy agreed, "and here's the other tip I wanted to share:

SECOND, IT'S A PERK IF THE INVESTMENT COMPANY FEES ARE ALIGNED WITH YOUR INTERESTS

There are only certain structures that are allowed to use this approach. I call it a 'hurdle.' Think of it this way: would you rather have an investment that charges you 3% per year no matter what they earn or an investment that charges you 1% a year plus a portion of the gains over a certain amount?

For example, let's say the investment company receives 15% of any gains beyond a hurdle of 6% for the year. So, if the investment has no gains for the year, the fee is 1%. Let's say the investment makes 16% in a year. Then management earns their 1% fee as well as 15% of the 10% gain over the 6% hurdle, which is another 1.5%. So they made 2.5%."

Dick jumped in, "That sounds awesome! The more I make, the more you make. What's not to like about that?"

Tommy smiled. "Exactly. It doesn't guarantee success, but it definitely aligns management with you.

Alright - that is everything I wanted to cover. As I mentioned, I know it would be beneficial for SuperRetirementPlanner to discuss this specific to you and your needs rather than for me to talk about it from my view."

"That makes total sense," Dick replied in a calm tone, "Okay, so let's see, we've met Lady Longevity, the Invisible Enemy, Evil Uncle Sam, Sarah Self-Pay, and now Iceberg Ivan. You said there were seven retirement villains, so I guess we've still got two more we need to deal with. I don't know about y'all, but I'd love to hurry up and meet these two and get out of this hot sun!"

END NOTES

1. www.statista.com/statistics/255518/mutual-fund-assets-held-by-investment-companies-in-the-united-states/

Chapter 7

Is *This* the Biggest Lie of the Brokerage Industry?

"Retirewent: what happened to the retirement hopes and dreams of Americans after the meltdown."

- Gregory Salsbury, Ph.D., *Retirementology*

Dick, Jane, and Tommy hopped out of their patio chairs and went inside. Dick wasn't alone. Not only were they all eager to keep moving through the retirement villains, but the hot summer sun had become virtually unbearable since Iceberg Ivan had left.

Dick and Tommy headed straight for the living room and picked out a couple of comfortable chairs – Dick naturally in his favorite recliner. Tommy faced him on a loveseat. Jane joined them a few minutes later with some lemonade and glasses she had grabbed from the kitchen.

"Oh, Jane, thank you so much!" Tommy said when Jane arrived.

Jane was happy to do something for Tommy. "Tommy, it's the least I can do. You've helped us so much in such a short amount of time. I'm starting to feel like we finally understand this stuff."

Tommy smiled. "I'm so glad to hear that, Jane, but remember, we still have two more retirement villains to meet. Don't get cocky on me!" Tommy enjoyed sharing such valuable information with his friends and couldn't help teasing Jane just a little.

Jane recognized the smirk on Tommy's face. "Don't you worry, Tommy. We're ready for the next two." She finished pouring the three drinks, handing one to both Tommy and Dick and took a sip for herself. "Alright," she said while putting her glass down and picking up her pen and pad of paper, "Who's next?"

Tommy leaned toward them. "Very well. I feel I should warn you. I know I've said that each of the villains is important. But this particular villain is extremely sneaky and could wipe out an entire nest egg. Oh, and don't be alarmed when he gets here."

Dick and Jane looked at each other. "Don't be alarmed," Dick said, "sounds like this retirement villain is going to be something else!"

At that exact moment, a cloud of smoke appeared in the middle of the living room. Dick, Jane, and Tommy kept their eyes focused on the smoke. As it faded, they could all see the next retirement villain. Even though Tommy had warned them, Dick and Jane were indeed alarmed; because standing before them was a wolf!

"Guys," Tommy quickly started, "I told you do NOT be alarmed. He can ruin your nest egg but doesn't physically bite you! Allow me to introduce your next retirement villain, Systematic Sammy."

Systematic Sammy was indeed an intimidating presence. He stood on his hind legs, was very muscular, and, most importantly, had an evil grin.

"Pleasure to meet you!" Systematic Sammy started, "Let me tell you a little about myself. As Tommy said, my name is Systematic Sammy. Yes, I am a wolf, and Tommy is right. I don't physically hurt you. Instead of crushing you in my jaws, I love to crush your nest egg!"

Dick and Jane were letting this sink in. As shocking as some of the retirement villains had been, none had been this physically frightening. Dick could sense that while Jane intellectually understood that Sammy wasn't going to attack them, she was still frightened.

Dick was eager to get this encounter over with. "Alright, let's move this along. What does Sammy represent, and how can he hurt us?"

Tommy nodded. "Good idea. Let's get right to it. First, what does he represent? Systematic Sammy represents a particular type of financial advice. Imagine that your advisor invests your money in the stock and bond market. After you retire, your advisor recommends you keep your investments the same and take money out of your nest egg each month to live off of. That type of withdrawal is called systematic. With me so far?"

Dick and Jane nodded.

"Great," Tommy continued, "This villain is a wolf because wolves are notorious for being something different than they appear. Of course, you've heard stories of wolves dressing in sheep's clothing to trick the sheep."

"Hey!" Systematic Sammy interjected, "I resent that analogy – I don't attack sheep!"

"I know, I know," Tommy said, "Bear with me." Tommy turned his attention back to Dick and Jane. "A sheep appears harmless, right? That's the same as taking a withdrawal once a month out of your nest egg. It seems logical, right? However, it's really a wolf in sheep's clothing. Taking a systematic withdrawal could actually wipe out your entire nest egg!"

"Wow," Jane finally gathered herself and joined the conversation, "That sounds horrible. I hope you have an example so we can better understand this."

Tommy looked at Systematic Sammy. "Okay," Systematic Sammy said, "I can take it from here. There are a couple of ways I can show you. Let me start with a straightforward example.

Assume you had $1,000,000, and you invested it for ten years. We'll assume you earned an average of 6% a year. Also, each year, you withdrew 6% a year. Okay, so you start with $1,000,000. Earn an average of 6% per year. Withdraw 6% per year. What would you have left at the end of the ten years?"

Dick and Jane looked at each other. "$1,000,000," they responded simultaneously yet hesitantly.

Systematic Sammy flashed a knowing smile. "Exactly. That's what everyone says, and that's why I'm compared to a wolf in sheep's clothing – because it's a trick question.

The trick to the question is that I didn't tell you that you would earn 6% every individual year. I said you would earn an *'average '*of 6% per year. If you **did** earn 6% each and every year, your answer would be correct, but if your return goes up and down each year but averages 6%, you may very well have an *extremely* different value at the end of ten years than $1,000,000.

Look at this handout I brought with me. (Figure 7.1) If you had a couple of poor investment years to start, solid investment years through year eight, and terrific investment years in the last two years, you would still earn an *average* of 6% per year. At the end of ten years, your $1,000,000 has fallen all the way down to $356,120. Yes, that's right; you earned an *average* of 6% per year, withdrew 6% per year, and managed to lose way more than half your money in only ten years!"

Is Average Return the Biggest Lie of the Brokerage Industry?

Year	Beginning Value	Withdrawal	Return	Ending Value
1	$100,000	- $6,000	- 30%	$65,800
2	$65,800	- $6,000	- 20%	$47,840
3-8		- $6,000	10%	
9	$33,828	- $6,000	20%	$33,394
10	$33,394	- $6,000	30%	**$35,612**

Figure 7.1

Dick was in complete shock. "That's unbelievable! It's just like you said, Tommy – it sounds so logical, but the person in this example is going to go broke! Why does that happen?"

Tommy opened his mouth to answer, but Systematic Sammy put his paw in front of it. "Tommy, I know you'll tell them anyway, and I'd rather it came straight from me. It boils down to this:

If you have your nest egg invested in anything that changes value – such as something tied to the stock and bond markets – that investment is probably changing in value at least once per day, but when you are retired, you need income every month; and for most people, that income is going to be the same every month. So, let's say your investments go down in value the first month you're retired. Are you willing to skip getting your income that month?"

"That's ridiculous," Dick quickly said, "you just said I'd be retired. We'd have to have that income to live on."

"Exactly," Systematic Sammy said, "So you're going to take your income, but your investments have lost value. That means you're forced into selling them when they are down. I'm sure you've heard the expression that you make money in the stock market by buying low and selling high, right?

Well, in this situation, you've bought high and sold low. It's the exact opposite of what you're supposed to do. As you can see from the simplified example we just covered, every single month your account drops, it forces you to sell lower than what it was worth the previous month.

Now, I've done such a successful job convincing people that this is a great idea that I bet even most financial advisors have bought in on my little plan. If most financial advisors fall into doing this for their clients, just imagine how many millions of retirees I can try to bankrupt!

In fact, I can give you a real-life example from print!"

The Most Dangerous Retirement Advice?

"Back in 2001," Systematic Sammy continued, "the *Miami Herald* had a certified financial planner that regularly contributed to the paper. In the December 2nd, 2001 edition, they printed this question and answer to and from the planner:

> *"Question: I am 70 years old and retired, hoping that my IRA would sustain me when the time came. Since I have to begin withdrawing next year, I would appreciate your advice. I was advised several years ago to invest my IRA in mutual funds. For a while it was great, but along with so many other people, I have lost a great deal in the last two years. Should I take my losses and reinvest in a secure savings even though the interest rates are low?*
>
> *Answer: If ever there was a time to stick with the plan, it's now. The ups and downs of the market are to be expected, and if you've been an investor for more than a few years, you've ridden a few waves yourself; mostly up markets, just no down markets this long and nasty. I feel your pain, but 2 percent CD's and no growth aren't going to cut it.*
>
> *Check your funds and make sure they're solid and leaning more to the conservative growth and growth income funds. Aggressive funds tend to be more volatile. Instruct your custodian to send you your required minimum distribution monthly by selling shares of your funds. This is called a systematic withdrawal and it works like a charm."*

"Oh my goodness!" Exclaimed Jane, "That's exactly what you told us was the wrong way to take money out!"

Systematic Sammy broke into a huge, devilish smile. "I know! It's absolute music to my ears! And as a retirement villain, it makes me so happy that investors believe that systematic withdrawals always work, *and* so do many financial salespeople."

Tommy wanted to jump into the conversation. "He's right. It's scary because that type of advice can be so dangerous. Before Sammy continues, I want to point something out. Let's look at one part of the article again":

"Instruct your custodian to send you your required minimum distribution monthly by selling shares of your funds. This is called a systematic withdrawal and it works like a charm."

This type of advice made Tommy angry. "This is flat out, completely and totally WRONG! Well, it's not 100% wrong," Tommy admitted, "Technically if the value of the funds *never* went down, the advice would be correct. Please let me know if you can find me a mutual fund that never goes down!

The phrase should have read: "This is called a systematic withdrawal, and it works like a charm as long as you have chosen the right mutual fund and the stock market always goes up faster than you are drawing the money out."

Dick laughed. "That's a good one! I wouldn't need a financial advisor if the stock market always went up!"

"Thank you!" Tommy was thrilled that Dick was just as irritated as he was. At this point, he realized he should settle down and let Systematic Sammy continue. "I'm sorry, Sammy. You can continue now."

Systematic Sammy, like all the other retirement villains, was in no hurry to explain all the ins and outs of systematic withdrawals for

Dick and Jane: "Sure. Listen to this quote from the book *Probable Outcomes* by Ed Easterling:

> *"Some advisors or planners will go so far as to advocate that today's long-term retirees invest heavily in the stock market. Those pundits say, "A market that has never lost money over thirty-year periods won't let you down in the future." It's true that there has never been a thirty-year period when stock market investors overall have lost money, yet there have been quite a few thirty-year periods that have bankrupted senior citizens who were relying upon their stock portfolios for retirement income."*

"And I'm happy to report," Systematic Sammy proudly summed up, "the reason the stock market has bankrupted retirees is the volatility of the market during times of withdrawals for income."

Tommy was watching Dick and Jane. They seemed to be following along quite well. While Systematic Sammy was still there, he wanted to ensure they covered one more topic.

• • •

How Risky IS the Market?

"Okay," Tommy started, "Let's cover one more thing. The reason a systematic withdrawal can harm you so badly is because stock and bond markets **are** volatile. So Sammy, please explain precisely *how* volatile the markets can be.

"You got it, boss!" Systematic Sammy said, "You need to understand two things: How volatile the markets can be, and how much that can affect you. Another quote from *Probable Outcomes* explains this well:

> *"During the period 1900-2009, the simple average of the annual gains for the stock market, excluding dividends, was 7.1%. The compounded*

annual gain excluding dividends reflects a more accurate view of realized annual returns at 4.7% over the 110 years.

The difference between the average return and the compounded return is the result of two effects denoted by Crest Mont Research as "volatility gremlins." These volatility gremlins can reduce the dollars you actually receive by more than 90%! By understanding their impact, investors can appreciate the benefits of reducing volatility and increasing the consistency of investment returns. Investors can then realize higher compounded returns, and experience a more enjoyable and less stressful investment ride."

"Let me update those numbers for you," Systematic Sammy said, "Through the end of 2022, so over 122 years, the stock market *average* annual return was 7.4%, while the *realized* annual return was 5.2%."[2]

Dick was both a little confused as well as upset. "That's what I thought you said! So whenever we see advertisements showing a great average return, that doesn't actually mean we'll earn that much money?"

Tommy nodded. "That's correct - unless your account earns exactly that return EACH year. The bottom line is how the author summarizes this section. Investors that can reduce volatility and increase the consistency of returns can realize higher compounded returns and enjoy a less stressful investment ride."

Jane chuckled, "Isn't that what everyone wants anyway?!"

Tommy laughed. "You're certainly not the only one. That's what Brenda and I want; I imagine most retirees agree! Keep going, Sammy."

"Very well," Systematic Sammy continued, "Here's a little more detail on how damaging volatility can be from *Probably Outcomes:*

"The first volatility gremlin is the impact of negative numbers on compounded returns. To illustrate the effect, consider an investment over two years. If an investment portfolio makes 20% the first year and loses 20% the second year, the simple average rate of return is zero. The investor, however, has actually lost 4%. To break even, it takes a greater positive return than the offsetting negative loss. For a -20% loss, the offsetting gain is +25%. It works the same whether the positive or the negative occurs first. A +25% gain can be wiped out by a -20% loss.

The second volatility gremlin is the impact of the range of returns on the average. As the returns in a series become more dispersed from the average, the compounded return declines. Keep in mind that half of all years in the stock market occur outside a 32% range, from -16% to +16%. As the level of dispersion increases, the impact from the second volatility gremlin increases".

Tommy didn't want Systematic Sammy to skip over this critical point. "So basically what the author is saying is, your goal should be to reduce losses, and if you can, eliminate them; and I'm sure you can imagine, Mr. Easterling isn't the only person making that recommendation. In fact, the man whom many would consider the most successful investor of the past 50-plus years, Warren Buffet, has said:

"Rule No.1 is never lose money.

Rule No.2 is never forget rule number one."[2]

"I hate that one," Systematic Sammy said, "Here's another quote – this one is from author Edward Winslow in his book *Blind Faith: Our Misplaced Trust in the Stock Market, and Smarter, Safer Ways to Invest:*

"The primary objective of an intelligent investment strategy should be to preserve capital and build upon it at a consistent, moderate rate in both bull

and bear markets. Our personal definition of risk is simple and understandable: we don't want to lose money."

"Oh, and let me give you one more quote from the previously mentioned *Probable Outcomes:*

Too often, investors have been led to believe that hope and faith in the long term are appropriate investment strategies. Investments should seek to make money, not simply to passively participate in the markets. Toward that end, the first rule of making money is to avoid losing money. Risk management is not just about enhancing success; it is about avoiding the unacceptable failures.

"Finally," Systematic Sammy summarized, "here's another helpful quote. This one is from best-selling author Harry S. Dent in his book *The Great Depression Ahead:*

"The key insight is not to accept the proposition that investors cannot, or should not, take steps to guard against losses. As an investor, it is your money, your future, and your responsibility to protect yourself in the best way possible."

Dick looked at Jane and grabbed her hand, "Okay, I think it's safe to say that all makes complete sense to us."

Tommy nodded and smiled, "I thought you might say something like that. There's one more topic I'd like Sammy to cover. While certainly no one can predict what the stock market will be like in the future, Sammy, please give us a quick rundown on what some economic experts are saying."

Tommy had just about pushed Systematic Sammy over the edge. "Tommy, I will cover that, but nothing more!"

Tommy nodded at Systematic Sammy and then smiled at Dick and Jane.

Systematic Sammy began on this final topic, "Alright, let's get this over with. I'll summarize many expert opinions with one in which I know SuperRetirementPlanner has confidence. Best-selling author Antti Illmanen published *Investing Amid Low Expected Returns* in April of 2022 and had this to say about expectations in the near future:

> *While we should be humble about predicting returns, I believe that the next ten years will be characterized by low realized returns. Having essentially borrowed returns from the future through multi-decade windfall gains, we are in for low returns for the next decade or longer. Yet, it is not clear whether the low returns will materialize through slow pain (persistent low income) or fast pain (repricing toward lower valuations and higher prospective returns)."*

"Slow pain or fast pain – that sounds like a terrible choice – especially when trying to live off of your nest egg!" Dick exclaimed.

"I agree," Systematic Sammy said, making his best effort at being *Sympathetic Sammy*.

Tommy interrupted again, "Sammy, I don't want you to skip anything important. So how do the experts suggest investors plan for this?"

Systematic Sammy snarled and took a step towards Tommy. Fortunately, Tommy had seen this before and knew Sammy couldn't physically hurt him, so he stood his ground. Systematic Sammy glumly responded, "Here's a quote from Ed Easterling's book *Probable Outcomes*:"

> *Secular bear markets are not periods during which to avoid investing; they are periods that demand an adjustment to investment strategy. The implication for today's investor is that the likelihood of financial success in retirement is considerably less than most pundits advocate.*

Systematic Sammy savored the last sentence. "That's right, the likelihood of financial success in retirement is considerably less than most pundits advocate. Doesn't that have a great ring to it?"

"Sammy!" Tommy yelled as he was losing patience.

"Alright!" Systematic Sammy said, "Here's what Mr. Easterling recommends for retirees in the same book:"

> *"Retirees who want to withdraw 5% or more will need a more consistent and higher return profile for their investments than passive investments in the stock market or bond market can provide. The principles of absolute return investing are important for preserving capital and generating much-needed returns."*

"Once again, the author is advocating avoiding losses. By "absolute return investing," Mr. Easterling is referring to seeking investments that don't lose value. Now, let's lastly look at the author's comments for those getting ready to retire:"

> *"Near-Retirees (within a decade or so of retiring) will be called Late Accumulators. The appropriate strategy for investors in this group needs to start with assumptions based upon reasonable expectations. The stock market is not positioned to start a secular bull ascent or achieve even historically average returns. This group of people has a sobering near future, one that requires wealth preservation rather than wealth accumulation. In a decade or two, this group will likely realize solid returns from the next secular bull market – the goal is to have all, or more, of their current savings available to invest. Great returns generated from half as much capital can still deliver a disappointing lifestyle in retirement."*

"I don't care what you all think about it, but come on, 'this group of people has a sobering near future' – isn't that the best?!" Systematic Sammy would not miss one last chance to take a jab at them.

"Enough already!" Tommy exclaimed, "Sammy, get out of here!" Before Systematic Sammy could respond, a cloud of smoke enveloped him, and he disappeared.

Dick was relieved to have Sammy gone. "Thank you! Okay, we get it. Systematic withdrawals from accounts that can lose value and taking too much risk with our nest egg can be dangerous. Plus, some experts believe the coming years could include some significant risk in the stock market. So is the solution to take all our money and put it into CDs? Or a savings account? Or better yet, how about under our mattress!"

Tommy knew Dick was frustrated, but he also detected a twinkle in his eye while he was talking. "Dick, I'm glad you can laugh a little at this. To answer your question, no, you don't need to put all your money under your mattress, and I know you're eager to hear some better solutions. I have to ask you for just a little bit of patience. You see, we'll get into some possible solutions when we meet our final retirement villain."

"Okay," Dick said, "I can live with that. But why do I have to be patient? Why don't you call up the last villain right now?"

Tommy smiled. "Well, he doesn't make house calls, so we have to go to him, but if you're interested, we can go see him right now. It's only about a 10-minute drive."

Dick and Jane responded in unison, "What are we waiting for?"

END NOTES

1. www.crestmontresearch.com/docs/Stock-Average.pdf
2. wikiquote.org/wiki/Warren_Buffet

Chapter 8

Is There a Better Way to Invest?

Creative thinking may simply mean the realization that there is no particular virtue in doing things the way they have always been done.

– Rudolph Flesh

Within minutes, all three were in Dick and Jane's Camry and on the road.

"So where are we heading?" Dick asked as he started his car.

Tommy couldn't help smiling because he knew what the follow-up question would be. "The museum of American history."

"Why in the world would we go there?" Jane asked before Dick could.

"I knew you'd ask that!" Tommy replied, "It's a pretty simple answer – that's where our last retirement villain is, and rather than ruin the surprise, why don't we just leave it at that until you meet him?"

Dick started to object but decided it wouldn't do any good. Besides, it wasn't far away. Throughout the drive, he racked his brain trying to remember the exhibits in the museum - which he hadn't seen for years.

They quickly arrived at the museum. Dick paid for their admission, and they made their way into the exhibits. "Alright, I give up. Who is it?"

Tommy chuckled at Dick's urgency. "Thank you for your patience! He's actually right behind you."

Dick and Jane quickly turned around. They saw an exhibit from the days of cavemen. Several men were around a fire pit - not real men of course, but mannequins.

"I don't get it," Dick said, "Come on out, retirement villain!"

The obligatory cloud of smoke immediately appeared, enveloping the exhibit. When the smoke settled, a man dressed in nothing but a loincloth greeted Dick and Jane with a series of loud grunts.

Even after meeting all the other retirement villains, Jane was startled. "Wait a second. Aren't you the mannequin?"

"Andy," Tommy calmly answered, "I'll take this. Dick and Jane, let me introduce you to your final retirement villain. His name is Antiquated Andy. Please understand that Andy is a caveman and can't talk for himself. Oh, and don't worry about his club. He isn't here to hit you with it. He's here to represent the damage he can do to your nest egg."

"Okay," Dick started, "I'm definitely sensing some symbolism here. Andy is Antiquated. We must be dealing with something old?"

Tommy let out a belly laugh. "Nicely done, Dick. You're absolutely right. Andy represents big brokerage investment advice that, for some brokers, hasn't changed for many generations. The world is undergoing massive change, and their advice stays the same. Investors needs go through significant change throughout their lives, yet the advice from these brokers stays the same. I'm sure you can see that this type of advice could be dangerous! So, since Andy can't help us, let me go ahead and give you the whole story.

Have you ever owned a brokerage account? Have you ever met with or worked with a stockbroker? There's an incredibly high chance that regardless of who the broker was or what company they worked for, I have a pretty good guess at what they recommended that you invest in.

Don't get me wrong: I'm not saying that all brokerage firms are bad, and I'm not saying that all stockbrokers are evil. Not at all. I *am* saying that some brokerage firms and brokers haven't changed their advice much over the past 100 years.

In these antiquated allocations, they typically recommend you invest in one of three places:

1. U.S. Stocks
2. U.S. Bonds
3. Cash

Now, I say one way or another because there are all kinds of ways to invest in those three areas: individual securities, mutual funds, ETFs, and all other sorts of options. But they're all usually made up of those three things. And guess what? Those are the same three things some brokers were selling decades and decades ago!

The good news about this Wall Street approach is that it works…sometimes. It works assuming the following three conditions:

1. The economy and stock market are generally doing well. You know, like much of the '80's and '90's.
2. You have enough time to ride out any downturns, and
3. You aren't drawing income off the account. I'll assume you haven't forgotten about Systematic Sammy already, right?!

It should be clear that this approach could be hazardous to your retirement!

Fortunately, there is a time-tested approach that could be a much more retirement-friendly way for you to invest. The method I'm referring to is often called the Modified Endowment Strategy of investing. This name stems from numerous college endowments that have popularized this style.

It's called a modification of the endowment strategy because we don't have billions of dollars to invest like some endowments! Since implementing this style in the '80s, these endowments have shown a remarkable ability to generate above-average returns while typically enjoying much fewer losses than the stock market.

In their November 13th, 2017 study titled, "Investing Like the Harvard and Yale Endowment Funds," Michael W. Azlen, CAIA, and Ilan Zermati noted:

> *US Endowment Funds have consistently achieved superior investment returns. This is especially the case for the "Super Endowments" of Harvard and Yale. They have achieved an average 20-year annualized return of 11.5%, 5.4% greater than the returns of a traditional 60/40 equity/bond portfolio.*

Andy, you remember the market meltdown of 2000 through 2002. Was your strategy able to bankrupt some retiree's nest eggs?"

Andy got *really* excited. A huge smile came to his face. He tossed his club down on the ground and started pounding his chest, jumping up and down and grunting loudly. Dick and Jane both took a couple of steps back out of shock.

Tommy had to stop him quickly. "Andy, enough! I'm sorry about that, y'all. Sometimes I forget that he can act like a caveman. Okay, back to the facts. Check out this first handout. Through the Harvard endowment's fiscal year 2010, it had easily returned better than a portfolio comprising 60% stock market and 40% bond market holdings. Of course, this comparison assumes the investor earned the returns of the stock and bond market indexes, and Iceberg Ivan showed you how unlikely that would be!

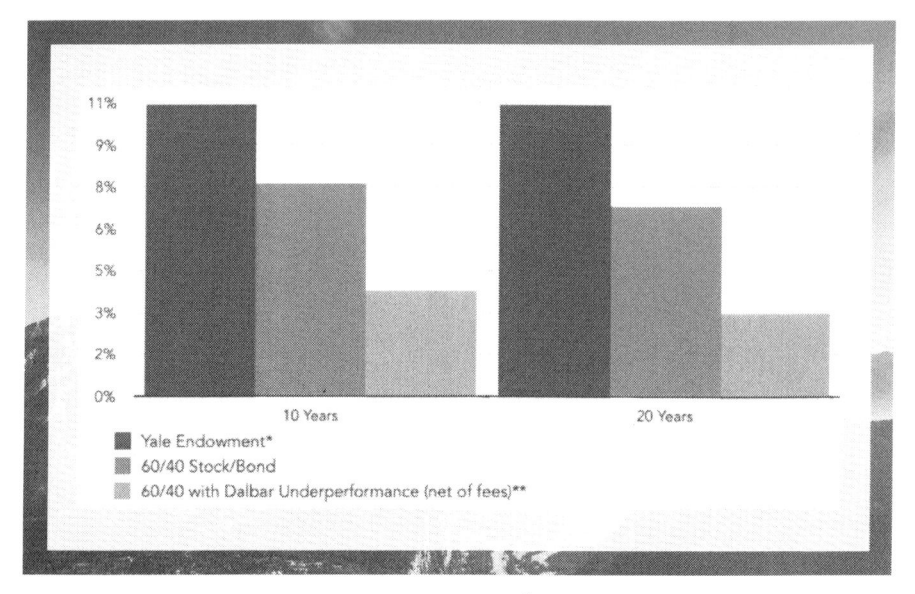

Figure 8.1[1]

So, the endowment returns during that period were excellent; but before jumping into such a strategy, there are two questions we should answer. The first is: can we duplicate their strategies? Let's go back to Mr. Azlen and Mr. Zermati's previously mentioned paper:

> *The US Endowment Funds are exceptionally well resourced and have access to the best fund managers and private equity programs, which contributes significantly to their investment success. However, in this paper we demonstrate that by adopting similar assets allocation principals, it is possible for smaller investors to obtain high levels of risk-adjusted returns for their own portfolios; superior to that of traditional equity/bond portfolios.*

These comments may not seem like a big deal, but they are game-changers. You see, *some* of the assets the endowments invest in were difficult to impossible for the typical investor to take advantage of for decades, but that has changed.

The second question for us to answer is: is this approach too risky? Listen to this quote from Jack Meyer, who managed the Harvard endowment from 1990 to 2005:

> *"The most powerful tool an investor has working for him or her is diversification. True diversification allows you to build portfolios with higher returns for the same risk. Most investors are far less diversified than they should be."* [2]

Ah! So, Jack Meyer claims better returns without additional risk. Doesn't this sound too good to be true? I don't blame you. After all, that's how investing is supposed to work: Low risk, low return. Higher risk, potential for higher returns.

And listen to this from David Swensen, the Chief Investment Officer at Yale from 1985 to 2021:

> *"Most investors, institutional and individual, are far less diversified than they should be,"* he says. *"They're way overcommitted to U.S. stocks and marketable securities." If you haven't been following the Ivies' investment strategies over the years, you may be surprised by how Harvard and Yale allocate their endowment assets. Their portfolios are most likely radically different from yours, or from the models advocated by most financial planners, which are still heavily weighted toward traditional asset classes like stocks, bonds, and cash. What's most striking about their portfolios today is how little they have invested in U.S. stocks and bonds.* [3]

This section sheds some light on the situation. The claim is a better opportunity for higher returns without more risk. So, the endowments are clearly doing something different. And what are they doing? Some might call it radical. I'd say so. After all, many on Wall Street have told us for generations that investing in stocks, bonds, and cash is the path to success. Yale and Harvard have defied Wall Street; and some claim they have proven Wall Street wrong!

The idea of enjoying true diversification is worth diving into more detail. Swensen writes extensively about this subject in his book, "Unconventional Success":

> *In spite of nearly universal support among investment professionals for well-diversified portfolios, market practice generally fails to reflect fundamental portfolio management precepts. Consider the average asset allocation of college and university endowments, which represent the best managed of institutional funds. Ten years ago (1993) domestic equities constituted nearly 50 percent of assets (48.6%) and domestic bonds more than 40 percent (40.8%). With two asset classes accounting for almost 90 percent of assets, the portfolios flunk the test of diversification. In the early 1990s, college and university endowment managers earned dismal grades.*
>
> *Contrast the experience of the broad group of colleges and universities with the best-endowed educational institutions. Harvard, Yale, Princeton, and Stanford lead the endowment world in size and led the endowment world with early adoption of well-diversified portfolios.*

In his book, Swensen shows the breakdown of investments held by these four esteemed endowments. On average, on June 30, 1993, they held over 44% of "diversifying assets." Fast forward to June of 2020 – 78% of the Yale endowment was invested in diversifying assets; and incredibly, only 2.3% was invested in the U.S. stock market! That's a night-and-day difference from most portfolios! In his book, Swensen summarizes this way:

> *The well-diversified portfolios produced superior results. Real-world application of fundamental investment principles produces superior outcomes.*

Endowment investing is not theory. Yale and many other endowments have been using these strategies going back as far as 1985.[4] The returns since then, and reduction of ups and downs are proof. Academically and with actual portfolios, the endowments have had proven success. Let's go back to the comments about Harry Markowitz. He published his work on diversification in 1959, which has had an enormous effect on investing ever since.

Unfortunately, Wall Street often uses Markowitz's research to recommend U.S. stock, bond, and cash portfolios and nothing else. Maybe these recommendations were made years ago because there were no cost-effective ways to use additional diversification back then. Or maybe Wall Street had different reasons…or motives.

Regardless, why does Wall Stree continue to make the same recommendations for the past 100 years? Laziness? Ignorance? Greed? All of the above? Author Raymond J. Lucia, CFP, has an opinion in his book *Buckets of Money*:

> *Why does Wall Street gravitate toward the asset-allocation method? The answer is actually quite simple. It's simple, profitable for the firm, and easy to implement. It's easy to charge a wrap fee on 100 percent of a client's assets."*

Dick and Jane had been very quiet. By spending so much time with the retirement villains, they had learned much more when they kept their mouths shut. At this point, however, they sensed that Tommy had reached a natural break in his explanation.

Dick asked what he thought was an obvious question, "So if they aren't investing in U.S. stocks and bonds, just exactly *what* are they investing in?"

Tommy smiled because he was happy that Dick had asked such a good question: "This handout shows a recent snapshot of the

Harvard Endowment Fund's holdings. Of course, their investments are constantly changing, but this gives you a general idea.

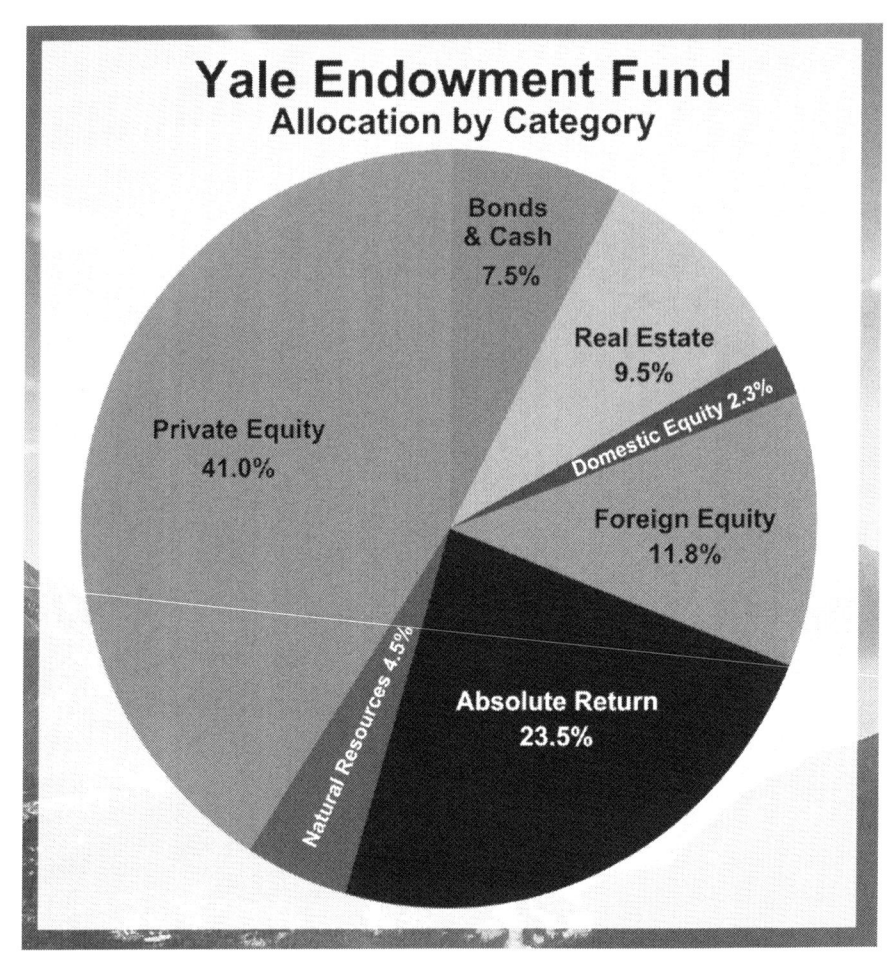

Yale Endowment Fund
Allocation by Category

- Bonds & Cash: 7.5%
- Real Estate: 9.5%
- Domestic Equity: 2.3%
- Private Equity: 41.0%
- Foreign Equity: 11.8%
- Absolute Return: 23.5%
- Natural Resources: 4.5%

Figure 8.2[5]

In this particular example, the endowment fund is only holding 26% of its assets in those three traditional areas:

1. U.S. Stocks: 11%
2. Bonds: 13%

3. Cash: 2%

Before we get into some of their other holdings, we should spend a moment on *why* the endowment doesn't invest more in these areas. Bonds, in particular, are an area where Harvard's David Swensen speaks passionately. The following is also from his book "Unconventional Success":

"Unfortunately for investors, corporate bonds contain a variety of unattractive characteristics, including credit risk, illiquidity, and callability.

Callability poses a particularly vexing problem for corporate bond investors. The holder of corporate bonds faces a 'heads you win, tails I lose' situation. If rates decline, the investor loses the new high-coupon bond through a call at a fixed price. If rates rise, the investor holds a now low-coupon bond that shows mark-to-market losses.

The best outcome for holding bonds to maturity consists of receiving regular payments of interest and return of principal. The worst outcome represents default without recovery. The asymmetry of limited upside and unlimited downside produces a distribution of outcomes that contains a disadvantageous bias for investors."

Tommy had to laugh. "Okay, I'll admit it: Mr. Swensen tends to dress up his language slightly more than I do! Here's how I'd sum up that last paragraph: Mr. Swensen believes corporate bonds, in general, provide too many risks and offer too few benefits. Below is how Mr. Swensen sums up his thoughts on bonds:

"Investment-grade corporate bonds, high-yield bonds, foreign bonds, and asset-backed securities contain unattractive characteristics that argue against inclusion in well-constructed portfolios."

That's pretty straightforward, and his comments make so much sense. Why should you bother to use bonds in your portfolio if they don't benefit you?

So, what types of investments DO the endowments typically invest in? Let's look at the categories listed in the Harvard Endowment handout we looked at a moment ago:

- Foreign Equity, which is 22% in Figure 8.2. This makes sense, right? While there are certainly unknowns overseas, it's difficult to argue there isn't opportunity.
- Private Equity, which is 13% in Figure 8.2. This category can be tougher for the individual investor to access but it could be a good fit for some. In short, private equity is investing in private companies. As it may sound, this can offer much greater potential returns as well as significant risk!
- Absolute Return, which is 16% in Figure 8.2. Absolute return generally means it keeps a priority on maintaining positive returns regardless of how the economy or stock market are doing. Sounds pretty logical, doesn't it? Many would argue this category is **far** more important to a retiree than it is to someone investing for retirement in their 20s or 30s.
- Real Assets, which is 23% in Figure 8.2. This is one of the most accessible categories for the individual investor to duplicate. Real estate, for example, can be invested in through multiple different methods and in relatively small amounts. Is it an important area to use in your portfolio? Once again, let's see what Mr. Swensen has to say in his book "Unconventional Success":

"High-quality real estate holdings produce significant levels of current cash flow generated by long-term, in-place lease arrangements with tenants. Sustained levels of high cash flow lead to stability in valuation,

as a substantial portion of asset value stems from relatively predictable cash flows."

This is an update from the 2019 Yale Endowment Annual Report:

"Investments in real estate provide material diversification to the Endowment. Twenty-year returns for the portfolio stand at 9.0% per annum."

You haven't forgotten about the Invisible Enemy already, right?" Tommy asked Dick and Jane.

Dick gave Tommy a knowing look. "Come on, Tommy, you know he made quite an impression on us. We won't forget everything he taught us about how dangerous inflation can be."

Tommy was glad to hear Dick's response. "Good! That's another reason some experts like including real estate in an investment plan. Here's one more quote from Mr. Swensen's *Unconventional Success*:

"With its inflation-sensitive nature, real estate provides powerful diversification to investor portfolios."

Well, that about sums up the areas I wanted to cover. I know Andy loves to be able to get out of the exhibit and stretch his legs, but I think it's time to send him back."

Dick and Jane smiled at Antiquated Andy, and Dick said, "Goodbye, Andy. It was nice meeting you, and even better, learning how to avoid your tricks!" Antiquated Andy got a confused look on his face and was instantly swept up in a cloud of smoke before he could do anything. After the smoke had cleared, Dick and Jane saw that Andy had returned to his place by the fire.

Jane was sad to see Andy go. "Tommy, Andy seemed so nice. Why did you get rid of him so fast?"

"I'm sorry, Jane," Tommy explained, "I love Andy, and it hurts to send him away. That's why I try to do it as quickly as possible. Plus, we've been through a lot together, and I still want to cover one last thought that should be important to you: is the Modified Endowment Strategy a good fit for retirees?

Well, certainly, the goal of achieving higher returns with less risk is appealing to everyone! So what's the catch? Generally, the Modified Endowment Strategy does not provide as much accessibility to your portfolio as the old Wall Street model. So, is that a problem for a retiree?

When you're retired, you need to be able to access *some* of your money! But I hope you're not planning to use *all* of your nest egg all at once, would you?"

Dick laughed. "If we use all our nest egg at one time, we'd have a pretty sorry -looking future, wouldn't we?"

Tommy nodded. "Exactly, and as we talked about with Systematic Sammy, most retirees want to create income with their savings and investments. Well, you'll never guess who else is doing that - the endowments! That's right, those universities are taking income from the endowments *every* year.

In fact, Ivy League schools rely on endowments to help fund more and more of their day-to-day operations. Incredibly, Yale is budgeting for 35 percent for their 2024 fiscal year and Harvard is budgeting 45% for their 2023 fiscal year![5, 6]

I don't know what that sounds like to you, but that sounds like a retiree using their nest egg to provide income to add to their Social Security and pension!"

"That makes a lot of sense," Jane said as she let everything they had just learned sink in. "Okay, so we've met all seven retirement villains, heard why they can be so dangerous, and discussed strategies to use against them. It feels strange that we don't have another one to expect to meet!"

"I agree, honey," Dick said, "Tommy, does that mean we're done?"

Tommy smiled. "Not exactly. I know we've been through a lot, but we have one last stop to make on the way back to your house."

END NOTES

1. http://www.news.yale.edu/2023/10/10/yale-reports-investment-return-fiscal-2023

2. www.spectator.co.uk/article/revealed-harvard-university-s-failsafe-investment-strategy/

3. "A League of Their Own." *SmartMoney*, September 26th, 2007, James B. Stewart
4. http://en.wikipedia.org/wiki/David_F._Swensen
5. www.yale.edu/funding-yale-home/overview-yales-budget
6. finance.harvard.edu/financial-overview

Chapter 9

YOUR Retirement Income Plan

"You can get poor a lot faster than you can get rich."

- Bob Miller

Tommy was excited about the surprise he had up his sleeve for Dick and Jane. As Dick drove, Tommy directed him from the back seat. First, he had him exit the highway in the big shopping area of Metropolis, but then he had him turn down the frontage road.

"Tommy," Dick wondered, "you've got to tell us what we're doing here!"

Tommy chuckled. "Dick, you just can't appreciate a good surprise, can you?"

Jane shook her head no and laughed. "Nope. Never has, and I'm quite sure never will."

Tommy told them to pull into a parking lot next to a one-story black building with a large metal facade in front of it. As Dick pulled into a parking spot, Tommy said, "Okay, let's get out quickly. I don't want us to be late for our meeting!"

"Meeting?" Dick and Jane asked inquisitively.

Tommy simply smiled as he led them to the front doors. He opened the door and smiled at the office manager, who was there to greet them.

"Hi, Margo," Tommy said, "How have you been?"

"Well, hello, stranger!" Margo replied, "It's great to see you!"

Tommy wasted no time making introductions. "Margo, I'd like to introduce you to my friends Dick and Jane. Guys, this is Margo. She basically runs the show around here!"

Margo smiled, "I don't know about that! Dick and Jane, it's so great to finally meet you! Tommy has told us a lot about you."

"Nice to meet you, Margo," Dick replied, "I hope most of what he's said has been good!"

"Absolutely!" Margo shot back quickly, "Now, you all are here for your meeting, right? You're right on time. Please follow me to your conference room."

Margo led them to a conference room and offered each of them a seat and a drink. "He'll be with you in just a minute," and she closed the door.

"He?" Dick questioned Tommy. Then he looked at Jane and said, "Am I the only one who's confused?"

Tommy was loving it, but he knew he finally needed to let them in on his surprise. "Okay, y'all. I set a meeting for us with SuperRetirementPlanner. I hope you're excited!"

"SuperRetirementPlanner?" Jane wondered, "Yes, we're obviously excited, but I never imagined we'd meet him in a regular office!"

As she was talking, the door opened, and a man walked in. "I know, I know," he said with a smile, "You were probably expecting a cape, tights, and for me to be flying through the sky, right? I'm SuperRetirementPlanner. Dick and Jane, I'm so pleased to meet you."

"It's great to meet YOU SuperRetirementPlanner!" Dick said as he and then Jane shook SuperRetirementPlanner's hand, "And yes, we were expecting something a little more, uh, more 'superhero-like.'"

SuperRetirementPlanner smiled. "I completely understand, and it happens all the time. I think the name throws people off. When it comes to your retirement, your planner doesn't need to look like a superhero – but they do need to help protect you from those nasty retirement villains! I trust Tommy took you on a journey to meet all seven of them?"

Dick and Jane nodded yes.

"Great!" SuperRetirementPlanner said, "Well, Tommy filled me in a little bit on your background. Normally, our first meetings are designed more for us to get to know all about your current situation and what you want your retirement to look like; but since it seems like you've got a time-sensitive situation, Tommy and I thought it would be best to spend a few minutes today jumping in on some details of creating retirement income. Then, we can get together another time to discuss all the details of your situation…without Tommy, of course!"

"That sounds wonderful," Jane said, "I'm glad I brought my pen and notepad – fire away!"

"Perfect," SuperRetirementPlanner started, "Alright, hopefully, you remember your time with Systematic Sammy, where you learned about one of the most common ways to take income in retirement that can *devastate* your retirement, and I *do* mean devastate. I'm sure you agree that if a strategy can take you from being retired to being broke, that is flat-out *devastating!*

Because of this, we believe that **Much of the Financial Services World Has Been and Continues To Do Retirement Income Planning WRONG!** Why do I say that? Listen to how I would describe the most common approach:

Step #1: Generate a masive stack of pages of colorful pie charts representing various asset allocation models. A stack so tall that a Philadelphia lawyer writing for the IRS would be impressed!

Step #2: At retirement, take a monthly systematic withdrawal from the portfolio.

Step #3: Hope the stock and bond portfolio does well enough so you don't run out of money.

Many financial advisors, stockbrokers, online calculators, and mutual fund companies do it this way. Now, I know you've already heard about the problems with this method. The great news is that there IS a better way to generate retirement income with the goal of making sure you don't run out of money.

We believe that the most essential step to a successful retirement is having a written retirement income plan. We call ours your Custom-Built Retirement Income Plan because we build them individually for every family we work with.

Now, before Tommy introduced you to the Seven Retirement Villains, you were probably like most people; you might hear about having a written income plan and think that it sounds like we're making a mountain out of a molehill, but hopefully after the last couple of days, you realize how important it is to build a plan to try to protect you from those villains."

Dick and Jane had been listening intently and were both nodding in agreement. Dick started, "Yep, that was me. I thought I had it all figured out. Now I realize how silly that was. I'm excited to get a plan in place to protect us from everyone we've met!"

Jane smiled, "Dick, that is music to my ears. I'm so excited for us to know what we're doing and not worrying about our money anymore."

SuperRetirementPlanner beamed, "Tommy, you have clearly done a fantastic job; thank you very much!"

Tommy appreciated the kind words. "That's very kind. Helping friends of mine retire with confidence has been possibly the most rewarding experience of my own retirement!"

"I love that," SuperRetirementPlanner responded. "Alright, let's get to it!

How We Create Your Custom-Built Retirement Income Plan

Before getting into the income-related action steps, we believe it is critical to remember what really matters most about your money. In fact, there is truly only one thing that really matters when it comes to your money: does it help you accomplish your goals?

I've been helping people with their money for over 26 years, and I've very rarely met someone whose goal was to get rich." Again, everyone nodded in agreement.

"One of my all-time favorite authors on investing is Dr. William Bernstein. He puts it perfectly in his book Rational Expectations:

The purpose of investing is not to simply optimize returns and make yourself rich. The purpose is not to die poor.

"Now, to be fair, I should never assume that I know your goal. So let me ask: is your most important goal to try to become rich, or is it never to be poor?"

Dick and Jane looked at each other. Jane said to Dick, "Honey, you better give him the right answer!"

Dick responded with a big belly laugh, "Oh dear, I may do silly things sometimes, but I'm no dummy! Our biggest goal is definitely never to be poor!"

"Smart man," SuperRetirementPlanner said with a smile. "Okay, great. So, we have the first step completed. The second step will sound straightforward. We list everything that you have that could possibly help make sure that you are never broke during your retirement.

Now, when most people hear that, they think only of their nest egg. But there are all kinds of resources that you might have. In addition to your nest egg, I would include your Social Security benefits, pension benefits, as well as additional items like equity in your home.

Now don't worry; I'm not planning on recommending you sell your house and live in a tent or anything like that! We simply want to make sure we are thorough and counting all of the resources available to you."

Jane was listening intently. "Those are great points. I certainly wouldn't have thought of all of those as retirement resources, but I can see how each of those can be helpful to us."

"Great," SuperRetirementPlanner continued. "The next step may also sound simple, but for some people, it can be very challenging. The next step is to decide how much income you need. You see, it will be difficult for us to make sure you never run out of money if we don't know how much of it you need every month!

Let me give you a couple of suggestions as you think about that question. First, it is up to you how you think about that number, but we've found it helpful for most people to think about it this way: if you retire today, how much money would you like to have coming in every month after taxes? That would be how much you would have available to spend every month. So, you don't have to worry about taxes, and you wouldn't need to worry about inflation. You leave both of those to us.

My second idea is optional. Some of our clients love this, and some don't really use it, but a second option is to break this number down into two different categories. The first is how much you **NEED** for your essential expenses, and the second is how much you **WANT** for your non-essential expenses."

Dick interjected, "But my non-essential expenses *are* needs!" He let out another belly laugh. Jane jabbed him with her elbow.

SuperRetirementPlanner smiled. "Believe me, I completely respect that! The reason some people like breaking their income into those two categories is that we can try to design it so that you have some kind of protection on the income you need for all of your essential expenses.

In that case, we would try to match your essential expenses with things like Social Security, monthly pension payments, or income from annuities with lifetime guarantees. That reminds me of another favorite quote about retirement.

Dr. David Babble was the Professor Emeritus at the Wharton School of Finance, and he has studied and written a great deal about retirement income planning. He ended up choosing this approach with his own retirement. When he wrote about this, he received many comments arguing that he had made foolish choices. The primary argument was that he should have put more of his money in the stock market to try to make more money. His response was:

'Let them criticize; let us sleep.'"

Jane's eyes lit up. "Oooh, I like that! All I want is to be able to sleep and to stop thinking about our money." Dick nodded in agreement.

"I completely agree," SuperRetirementPlanner said. "That will be our goal. Now, as we build your Custom-Built Retirement Income Plan, it will need to be able to do four things for you:

1

First, your plan needs to provide you with regular and dependable income every month. Now, when you hear that sentence, your initial response is probably, 'Well, duh!'"

Everyone chuckled, and Jane said, "Well…that sounds simple, but when you say dependable, that makes me think of Systematic Sammy. Maybe sometimes people think something is dependable, but unfortunately, they find out it wasn't dependable at all."

Dick and Jane were both curious to see SuperRetirementPlanner's response. He started with a broad smile and said, "Jane, I've just learned something…I just learned who the A+ student is around here! Well done!"

Jane was simultaneously proud to have answered correctly but was now also a little embarrassed. Dick smiled and put his hand on Jane's, "There is certainly no doubting that. She is definitely the superstar student in the room!"

SuperRetirementPlanner continued. "Jane, you are exactly right. When you met Systematic Sammy, you learned that systematically withdrawing from the stock market is not dependable. So, how do we create income from your nest egg?

We will get into those details in a future meeting, but at a basic level, we will typically separate your nest egg into three categories. I'll call them the growth, safe, and dividend categories. The first category would be growth investments like the stock market. It's not that you can't have money invested there in retirement. It's just that you don't want to count on that for your retirement income.

Next would be the safe category, which is money where the principal is guaranteed. A CD at a bank would be a simple example.

The last category would be dividend-paying investments. The goal for these would be to regularly pay dividends at good rates, which could be something like five, six, seven, or even eight percent."

"Hey!" Dick interjected, "That sounds a lot like that endowment stuff that Tommy told us about when we met Antiquated Andy! I really liked hearing about those."

SuperRetirementPlanner nodded, "That's correct, Dick. So, at its most basic level, to make your retirement income more dependable, we draw that income off the accounts in the safe category and from the dividends from the last category I mentioned.

A great example of this was when COVID hit in March of 2020. The U.S. stock market dropped around 33% in 33 days. Aside from all of the health and political issues of that time, imagine if you were retired and had all of your nest egg in the stock market at that time."

"Oh my goodness!" Jane remarked, "How could you even sleep?"

"Exactly," SuperRetirementPlanner said. "I'm happy to report two things about our clients during that crash. First, they all continued receiving monthly income, and second, they didn't have to panic about the stock market. That's because they knew that the stock market wasn't creating their monthly income."

2

"So we talked about the safe category and the dividend category, but we skipped over the growth category. Well, the second thing your plan needs to provide you with is an income that accounts for the effects of the invisible enemy so that you don't lose purchasing power over time.

That's where the growth category comes in. Most retirees will want at least a small amount of their nest egg invested in something that has the potential to grow quite a bit throughout their retirement.

The key is to give those investments time because their value will have ups and downs. This is where having a planner to watch over everything can be so helpful. Part of our job is to help you determine when and how to shift funds from one category to another.

3

The third thing your plan needs to do is to ensure that your money lasts as long as both of you do. We just discussed how that is the most important goal, right?"

Dick and Jane nodded in agreement, and SuperRetirementPlanner continued, "This is a step that we feel truly needs to be custom-built because every family's situation looks so different.

For example, we have clients who can pretty much live off of the Social Security payments. We have other clients where Social Security is just a tiny portion of how much they spend each month. Those differences can be because of all kinds of factors. So, ensuring their income doesn't run out will likely differ depending on the situation.

4

Fourth and finally, if one of you passes away before the other, our plan needs to be prepared to take care of the income for the surviving spouse. We feel that our industry often ignores this because it's not a fun thing to think about.

Unfortunately, a spouse passing away can affect many different pieces of your retirement income. It will reduce the total amount of Social Security you're receiving. It could reduce the amount of pension income you're receiving, and it can increase the amount of taxes you're paying.

It's not fun to talk about, but what if Dick were to pass away a few years after we implement your income plan?"

Dick and Jane looked hesitantly at each other. Dick said, "Well, you're right that it's not fun to talk about; but the most important thing is that I would want to make sure that Jane would be okay."

"Exactly!" SuperRetirementPlanner said, "And that's why it needs to be part of our plan. The goal is that you would know it is in place so that you don't have to worry about it."

Jane smiled, "Not worrying about money. That is my other goal besides never being poor."

SuperRetirementPlanner nodded in agreement. "Well said, Jane. Alright, let's stop there. I know you've had an exhausting couple of days, but most importantly, I haven't learned all the details of your situation. So, the next time we talk, we'll dig into your specific information.

Once we have all that, our team's job is to build your Custom-Built Retirement Plan, which will include allocating your nest egg and how you should create your retirement income.

"Wow!" Jane interrupted, "After meeting Lady Longevity and the Invisible Enemy of inflation, I was definitely worried about running out of money. Just hearing how you will build our plan gives me so much hope!"

SuperRetirementPlanner always enjoyed hearing his clients have hope. "Thank you, Jane. It's certainly not a guarantee, but it's our goal. So that's a quick overview of your Custom-Built Retirement Income Plan. We want it to be as much like your current paycheck as possible!"

Dick felt the urge to jump in, "I would think that would be what just about anybody would want as they get ready to retire." Everyone in the room nodded, and Dick continued, "Tommy, thank you SO much for everything you've done for Jane and I. We will never forget it. SuperRetirementPlanner, thank you SO much for spending your valuable time with us. I am sure that Jane agrees with me when I say, what do we need to do to get moving on our retirement plan? I think we are both very excited to be retiring with confidence!"

Tommy blushed at Dick's warm words. "You're very kind, and you're welcome. As I mentioned before, it may be my favorite part of retirement! And SuperRetirementPlanner, I'd also like to thank you for your time."

"You're all very welcome," SuperRetirementPlanner said, "It's also so gratifying for us! Dick, as far as your question goes, on your way out, please schedule a meeting with Margo. She will let you know all the documents we'll need you to bring so that we can begin putting together the best plan possible for you.

Oh, and I have one more piece of homework for you. Let me give you this report I've put together - I'd like you to read it before our next meeting. I call it *'Ten Steps to Helping You Save YOUR Retirement.'* It gives you some simple ideas I'd like you to be familiar with before we begin working together."

"Sounds terrific!" Dick replied, "There's no way Jane or I will fall asleep tonight before we finish reading it!"

SuperRetirementPlanner smiled. "Wonderful. It's been an absolute pleasure meeting both of you. We look forward to seeing you soon, and most importantly, we look forward to helping you retire with confidence!"

Chapter 10

Save YOUR Retirement!

Finertia: paralysis by analysis brought on by trying to comprehend contradicting and confusing financial information.

– Gregory Salsbury, Ph.D. in his book *Retirementology*

I hope you enjoyed joining Dick and Jane on their journey. But what about you? Do you have your very own SuperRetirementPlanner? One of the greatest challenges of dealing with your finances is finding the right person and team to help you. The report SuperRetirementPlanner gave Dick and Jane could help you find the right fit for you:

• • •

10 Steps to Helping You Save *YOUR* Retirement:

Step 1: Don't Go It Alone!

If you've made it this far, you know that we believe in the value of having a team working with you. The rules of the game are constantly changing. You need trusted guides who focus on solving these particular types of financial problems. These trusted guides won't be found in the form of your favorite bank teller, nor at the local coffee shop or beauty shop. The greatest protection available will be with specialized teams of professionals who will help you build and manage the plans covered in this book.

Step 2: Beware of a 'planner' that will help you implement investments if no plan is prepared.

Buying financial products without a plan is like having surgery without an exam. A doctor who performs surgery without an exam would be malpractice!

The same holds for a financial advisor who sells a product without an analysis. If you remove the planning process, you are left with nothing more than a product salesperson.

Now, a plan may be many things. It can be a short one-pager, all the way up to a thick set of charts and graphs. Even if the written plan is short, the interview process must not be.

The best planning is not due to the thickness of the plan but because of the depth of the interview. The planner must ask about all your issues, not just the ones he can make money on. For example, they should ask about your taxes, home financing, company benefits, insurance, estate planning, retirement goals, investments, etc.

A good advisor knows how to get to know you, your goals, and your fears. If you feel they truly understand your emotions, as well as your finances, then you may be with the right advisor!

Step 3: If the planner you're talking to charges a planning fee, ask how much of the fee must be paid in advance and if they cover a specific amount of time, such as 12 months, or if they cover the completion and implementation of your plan.

In my opinion, you are usually better off working with an advisor who charges their planning fees on a flat basis, no matter how many hours they spend with you or on your planning. Hourly charges can work, but I have seen many instances where disputes have arisen because of the number of hours being billed. I have also seen many cases where people felt there were too many hours being charged, then stopped the planning process because they thought it was running too much money -- thus prohibiting them from getting their planning finished.

Step 4: **Ask the planner you're talking to if they charge fees for managing some or all of your money instead of, or in addition to, planning fees and product sales commissions.**

Some financial advisors charge for money management (sometimes called asset management) services in various ways, almost always based on a percentage of the money they manage for you. These fees can range from 1 to 3 percent per year in most cases (including investment costs). So, the more money they are managing, the more the fees you'll pay.

This method of charging money management fees is not necessarily bad, but you should know how much the fees are, how they are billed, and what kind of discounts are available for larger accounts. While this structure can work, it is a lot more appealing for someone starting out investing as opposed to someone near or in retirement. You can quickly do the math on how much one to three percent of hundreds of thousands or millions of dollars is – every year!

Be sure to get clarification as to whether or not these money management fees are separate from financial planning fees. Some advisors will charge financial planning fees charge additional money management fees on top of the planning fees. With this type of advisor, ask them if you pay them for planning fees, if you will be required to use their money management services, or if you're free to invest your money based on their advice with any money manager you choose.

Some advisors will not charge you a planning fee and just charge the money management fees if you let them manage the money. You should ask if they do any financial planning *before* making money management recommendations. If they say they don't or give you some sales pitch instead of a plan, get out of there quickly! (Remember Step 3.)

Another method to watch out for is if the advisor charges a money management fee *in addition to* product sales commissions. Suppose you are expected to pay 1 to 3 percent of your money for management as well as paying fees for such things as mutual funds and variable annuities. In that case, your investment fees will almost certainly get expensive. Make sure you're clear on how this works.

One point I will add: I've had many people over the years tell me that they are uncomfortable asking a financial professional how they are compensated. I completely understand that this can be awkward. However, please understand a few things. First of all, the reason you need to ask isn't your fault, and it isn't their fault. It's the system. Financial professionals can structure their fees in so many different ways, many of which are difficult to understand and essentially invisible. Asking is the only way for you to know.

This is important. This is your money you're dealing with. It's also your retirement. You only get one chance to get it right.

Finally, if the financial professional is uncomfortable talking about how they are compensated or if they are offended at all, that is another huge red flag. You know darned well that no financial professional works for free, so why would they be uncomfortable talking about it? And if the question is brushed off, in my opinion, that is enough reason to look elsewhere.

Step 5: **If the planner charges fees, ask if they provide you with a written, 100 percent guarantee of unconditional satisfaction.**

If they are so sure they can help you, they should back up that promise with an ironclad guarantee. The benefits you receive must exceed the cost of the planning/advice. You are the only person who can determine the amount of help you have received, and the benefit received cannot be determined until the plan has been completed and presented to you. There should be no question in your mind that you have received more benefit than cost. If not, then the fee should be adjusted or returned.

(FYI: They **cannot** guarantee anything about any investments you decide to make through them. It is against the law for them to do so unless the product has written guarantees built into it.)

Step 6: **If the financial professional doesn't charge fees, make sure you have a clear understanding of how they are compensated.**

Generally, if they don't charge a planning fee and they don't charge an asset management fee, they are likely being compensated by commission. While our industry often considers 'commission' to be like a four-letter word, this type of professional isn't necessarily bad. However, it is critical that you reach a point in your relationship of trust. The last position you want to be in is questioning whether something is being recommended because it's the best thing for you or if it is being recommended because it pays a nice commission. This distinction is critical. It is the difference between finding your trusted advisor or dealing with a financial salesperson.

Take car shopping as an example. If I go to a Ford dealership, I know the salespeople there will try to sell me a Ford. They aren't trying to convince me that they are unbiased. They may help me figure out which Ford is the best car for me, but they aren't going to recommend that I head over to a Toyota dealership.

There's nothing wrong with salespeople. The problem is when someone holds themselves out as someone you should trust—especially for something as important as your finances. I know what I'm getting when I talk to a Ford salesperson. You need to figure out what you're getting when you deal with a financial professional who works by commission only.

Step 7: Beware of financial advisor 'employees'

If the advisor works *for* a brokerage house (Merrill Lynch, Smith Barney, Morgan Stanley, Wells Fargo Securities, etc.) or *for* an insurance company (John Hancock, MetLife, Northwestern Mutual, etc.), you want to be careful. They may still be the right person. However, you need to realize that these advisors almost always have limitations on what they can and cannot do. These limitations are dictated by their home office. And how much does their home office know about you?

As a result, while a particular planning strategy may be particularly valuable for you and your unique circumstances, an advisor with one of these organizations may be unable to help you due to home office driven limitations. And even if they can help you, their home office may not allow them (for various reasons that have nothing to do with you) to use the optimal financial vehicles for that strategy. So, be careful when dealing with someone who is not independent.

Step 8: **Beware of Online 'Resources.'**

Information online should be viewed with a very skeptical eye. Today, it is not uncommon for retirees and their children to get online to do research. The critical question should be, "Are you getting information from a credible source?" This can be very difficult to decipher online.

An additional problem is information overload. If you research the keywords "when should I claim Social Security" on Google today, you will find over 688 million articles, websites, and "resources" to review.

The problem is, before you finish your review of these 688 million resources, you could be dead without having followed through on any of the advice. Obviously, this would defeat your original planning goals. Now, you must do your due diligence and research, but be sure you're researching the right thing – getting the right help. Remember **Step 1 (Don't go it alone).**

Finally, remember the first lesson in Chapter 5: there is no such thing as an unbiased financial professional. Well, the same goes for online advice. Any time you see an absolute statement, it is due to a bias. Using common sense, do you think all of the following statements are really true?

- **No one** should ever place money into annuities.

- **Everyone** should defer their Social Security until age 70.

- The **only** type of life insurance **anyone** should own is term insurance.

- The stock market **always** beats other investments.

Of course, it would be impossible for anyone to prove such statements. Yet comments like these abound. Online information can be helpful, but don't forget about the author's bias.

Step 9: Demand Proof!

There is nothing worse than getting sold a bad idea. Slick talk can be very persuasive, but in the end, it may prove financially disastrous. When seeking professional advice, we recommend that you ask the following to ensure that you are being advised by an accomplished and experienced professional or team of professionals:

How do you invest in your professional knowledge? This question is a great way to gauge the prospective advisor and team's commitment to staying current on new laws, tax code changes, and cutting-edge ideas to help preserve and grow your wealth.

Ask about their recognized financial designations. Education is an essential ingredient in selecting a financial advisor team. An educated team of financial advisors will usually have at least one of the following credentials:

- CPA - Certified Public Accountant
- CFP - Certified Financial Planner
- ChFC - Chartered Financial Consultant
- CLU - Chartered Life Underwriter
- RFC – Registered Financial Consultant
- APFS - Accredited Personal Financial Specialist

The above organizations require that the professional pass an initial exam and obtain continuing professional education. By seeking a planner or advisor or team with one or more of the above designations, you can be reasonably assured that the team has committed to obtaining sufficient knowledge to excel in financial planning and consulting.

Step 10: Be Smart and Trust Your Feelings.

I'd love to tell you that our experience has taught us that, as human beings, we will make decisions based entirely on logic. But I can't. People are not wired that way.

We've all been taught to never judge a book by its cover – right? But that is precisely what we often do. It's okay to be attracted to professionals with well-designed materials. That shows pride. Frequently, the ones who appear to be the best really are!

Then, when you meet face-to-face, gauge your emotions. If you feel comfort and a sense of greater security, trust that feeling. Bring all the decision-makers in your family to meet the advisory team. If you all feel that the advice given was in line with their published message, and you all have more peace of mind at the conclusion of the meeting, then you've found yourself a good advisory team.

SAVE YOUR RETIREMENT!

Pat Strubbe Through the Years

December 1976 – A very young Pat has a frightening encounter with Santa!

1980 – Pat and his sister Betsy all dressed up at their grandparents farm before heading to church

October 2005 – Pat, Carter, and Ava meet Mickey for the first time.

December 2005 – Just after Carter and Ava complete their performance in the church Christmas pageant.

July 2009 – Pat, Carter, and Ava at the gorgeous San Francisco Giants AT&T Park – on vacation visiting Pat's sister.

January 2013: Pat, Carter, and Ava just before hitting the slopes in North Carolina on their church teen ski trip

June 12, 2011 – Pat and Janelle get married at First Evangelical Lutheran Church in Lake Geneva, Wisconsin. This had special meaning because it is the same church Janelle's parents were married in back in August of 1973.

June 2011 – Pat and Janelle honeymooning in Maui. This was taken at a beautiful unplanned stop on the highly recommended Road to Hana.

June 2012 – Pat and Janelle follow a conference in Miami with a weekend in Key West and try a tandem bike for the first time!

June 2012 – Wearing silly caps at DisneyQuest. Orlando is definitely a favorite Strubbe vacation stop!

March 2013 – The 'after' picture from the Strubbe's first time participating in The Color Run. As you can see, it was a lot of fun!

November 28, 2014 – The Strubbe family is blessed with Gabriella Madelynn Strubbe. She may be a planner as well since she was born on her due date. ☺

June 2015 – The first Strubbe family cruise, which sailed from Charleston to the Bahamas. Much fun was had and lots of food was eaten! ☺

June 2016 - Gabby meets Isla for the first time

Summer 2016 - A selfie before heading to a friend's wedding

Christmas 2016 - Our best-ever Christmas card photo

Christmas 2017 - Gabby and Isla are not too excited to get their picture with Santa!

Summer 2018 - Gabby and Ava trying out a side-ponytail

Summer 2019: Gabby and Isla fall in love with Sally from Peanuts at Carowinds

July 2020 - Janelle's sister Jamie gets married in the beautiful Great Smoky Mountains

Fall 2020 - Gabby helping dad with his radio show

Spring 2021 – Isla also helping dad with his radio show

May 2021 - Ava graduates USC with honors!

Thanksgiving 2021
Also celebrating Pat's parent's 50th anniversary!

2022 - Annual Christmas card picture

April 2023: Bucket list moment for Pat, his dad, and their friend Nick playing the Old Course at St Andrews.

SAVE YOUR RETIREMENT!

A Small Request

Thank You for reading Save Your Retirement!

I have a small, quick favor to ask. Would you mind taking a minute or two and leaving an honest review for this book on Amazon? Reviews are the BEST way to help others purchase this book and I would love some helpful feedback.

SCAN THE CODE BELOW
TO LEAVE A REVIEW!

If you have any questions or would like to speak to one of our retirement planners, give us a call at 803-798-1988 or email us at FrontOffice@SCPreservation.com. We would love to see how we can help you retire with confidence!

SCAN HERE
TO LEAVE REVIEW

803.798.1988   frontoffice@scpreservation.com

Watch us on TV!

THE MIDLANDS RETIREMENT REPORT

WIS-NBC SUNDAYS 7-8AM
&
WLTX-CBS SUNDAY 8-9AM

Pat is honored to be the financial expert on the Midlands Retirement Report, which is a quick, two-minute tip to help you with your retirement.

WATCH THE MIDLANDS RETIREMENT REPORT ON YOUTUBE

@PreservationSpecialistLLC

SAVE YOUR RETIREMENT!

Stay Tuned to our Radio Show!

TIPS TO MAXIMIZE. STRATEGIES TO PROTECT.

560 WVOC — SUNDAY 9-10AM
AND — SATURDAY 9-10AM
98.5 WOMG — SUNDAY 7-8AM

Did you know that Save Your Retirement is also a radio show and podcast?

Join Pat with his host, Jen Rezac, as they tackle today's biggest retirement issues.

If you can't tune in live to the show be sure to stream our podcast anytime to stay up to date on market news!

**STREAM OUR PODCAST AT:
SOUNDCLOUD.COM/
SAVE-YOUR-RETIREMENT**

Save-Your-Retirement

Also by Pat Strubbe!

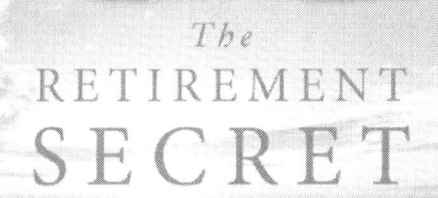

The RETIREMENT SECRET

A Simple Approach to Financial Peace-of-Mind

PAT STRUBBE

AVAILABLE NOW

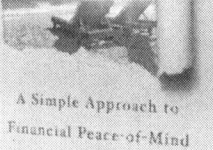

In The Retirement Secret, Pat introduces the three retirement mentors, teaching you how to understand your finances and plan your retirement before you get there.

If you're like most people, you're facing the looming specter of retirement on your own, in what Pat calls the do-it-yourself retirement system. You're not sure you'll ever have enough money to retire, and you're concerned that you won't know how to make that money last as long as it needs to.

The Retirement Secret will set your mind at ease, answering your questions in a fun, easy-to-read story that you won't want to put down.

theretirementsecret.com

Made in the USA
Columbia, SC
29 June 2025